ENCYCLOPAEDIA OF EMINENT THINKERS

VOLUME-VII: JAYAPRAKASH NARAYAN

Encyclopaedia of Eminent Thinkers Series

Vol. I.	The Political Thought of **Mahatma Gandhi**
Vol. II.	The Political Thought of **Nehru**
Vol. III.	The Political Thought of **Rabindra Nath Tagore**
Vol. IV.	The Political Thought of **Radhakrishnan**
Vol. V.	The Political Thought of **Vinoba**
Vol. VI.	The Political Thought of **Aurobindo**
Vol. VII.	The Political Thought of **Jayaprakash Narayan**
Vol. VIII.	The Political Thought of **Vivekananda**
Vol. IX.	The Political Thought of **Ambedkar**
Vol. X.	The Political Thought of **M.N. Roy**
Vol. XI.	The Political Thought of **Dadabhai Naoroji**
Vol. XII.	The Political Thought of **Veer Savarkar**
Vol. XIII.	The Political Thought of **M.A. Jinnah**
Vol. XIV.	The Political Thought of **Tej Bahadur Sapru**
Vol. XV.	The Political Thought of **C. Rajagopalachari**
Vol. XVI.	The Political Thought of **Subhas Chandra Bose**
Vol. XVII.	The Political Thought of **Mohammad Iqbal**
Vol. XVIII.	The Political Thought of **K.B. Hedgewar**
Vol. XIX.	The Political Thought of **Bhagat Singh**
Vol. XX.	The Political Thought of **M.S. Golwalkar**
Vol. XXI.	The Political Thought of **Sir Syed Ahmed Khan**
Vol. XXII.	The Political Thought of **Mahadev Govind Ranade**
Vol. XXIII.	The Political Thought of **Pandit Deendayal Upadhyaya**
Vol. XXIV.	The Political Thought of **Lokmanya Bal Gangadhar Tilak**
Vol. XXV.	The Political Thought of **Annie Besant**
Vol. XXVI.	The Political Thought of **C.R. Das**
Vol. XXVII.	The Political Thought of **Gopal Krishna Gokhale**
Vol. XXVIII.	The Political Thought of **Lala Lajpat Rai**
Vol. XXIX.	The Political Thought of **Maulana Abul Kalam Azad**
Vol. XXX.	The Political Thought of **Sir Pherozeshah Mehta**

About the Author

K.S. Bharathi did his Master's Degree in Gandhian Thought, Peace-Science, Economics, and political Science. He also did Postgraduate Diplomas in Politics, Public Administraion, Population Dynamics, Gandhian Thought, Tourism, and Telgu. He has contributed some articles in learned journals. He is the author of : *Foundation of Gandhian Thought Gandhi and Humanity, Socio Religious Thoughts of Mahatma Gandhi, The philosophy of Sarvodya, The Satyagraha of Mahatma Gandhi, Gandhi and Nehru, Foundatoins of Ambedkar Thought, The Social Philosophy of Mahatma Gandhi, Gandhian Approach to Rural Development, The Relevance of Gandhi, Gandhi and Vinoba, The Philosophical Foundations of Gandhian Thought, The Political Thought of Gandhi, The Economic Thought of Gandhi, The Social Thought of Gandhi* and *The Quintessence and Chronology of Gandhi*. At present, he is the Head of the Postgraduate Department of Gandhian Thought of Nagpur University. He is the Chairman of the Board of Studies of Gandhian Thought, member of the Academic Council, member of the Faculty of Social Science, member of the Board of Examination, and member of the Doctoral Research Committee of Nagpur University.

ENCYCLOPAEDIA OF EMINENT THINKERS

VOLUME-SEVEN

THE POLITICAL THOUGHT OF JAYAPRAKASH NARAYAN

K.S. BHARATHI
Head, P.G. Department of Gandhian Thought,
Nagpur University, Nagpur

CONCEPT PUBLISHING COMPANY PVT. LTD.
NEW DELHI-110059

ISBN: 978-81-7022-708-3 (Vol. 7)
ISBN: 978-81-7022-684-0 (Series)

First Published 1998

Published and Printed by

Concept Since 1974

Concept Publishing Company Pvt. Ltd.
A/15-16, Commercial Block, Mohan Garden,
New Delhi-110059 (India)
T : 91-11-41101460
E : publishing@conceptpub.com, *W*: www.conceptpub.com

TO
MY MOTHER

K. S. KUMARI BAI

PREFACE

There are many valuable books on Jayaprakash Narayan. There is hardly any book attempting a comprehensive exposition and evaluation of the Political thought of Jayaprakash Narayan. This work seeks to provide a comprehensive exposition of the Political Thought of Jayaprakash Narayan in a precise and lucid manner.

Jayaprakash Narayan struggled to achieve the noble ideals of justice, equality and freedom in order to contribute to the cause of social reconstruction. He was one of the greatest political thinkers that India produced in the twentieth century. He was against the system of parliamentary democracy and the institutions of ballot box and party system which make only mockery of democracy. He considered centralisation of political and economic authority as dangerous for establishing socialism. He had been in search of a political faith for the sake of freedom and human progress.

I would like to place on record my indebtedness to scholars and thinkers whose ideas enabled me to bring out this book. I gratefully acknowledge the scholars from whose work I have drawn citations viz. Dr. D. R. Bali, Dr. R.C. Gupta, Dr. Verinder Grover, Dr. V.D. Mahajan and Dr. Bhola Singh.

So far as the writing of this book is concerned, whatever success I have achieved is due to the relentless efforts and encouragement of my friend, philosopher and guide, Dr. P.S.G. Kumar, Head, Department of Library and Information Science, Nagpur University. I sincerely express my gratitude to him.

I express my warm thanks to Shri P. N. Hardas and Shri S. T. Patale of Gandhian Thought Department, Nagpur University, for their help and cooperation provided to me in the completion of this work.

I am indebted to Mr. Ashok Kumar Mittal, Concept Publishing Company for publishing this book in such a short span of time. Finally, I hold myself to blame for the errors and shortcomings if any. This work would have not been completed without the grace of Lord Venkateswara of Tirumala and Alamelu Thayar of Tiruchanur.

K. S. BHARATHI

CONTENTS

1

LIFE AND WORK OF JAYAPRAKASH NARAYAN

Life of Jayaprakash Narayan is a story of total dedication and service to the cause of common man in India. His compassionate heart and humanist outlook yearned to see mankind in the state of peace, happiness and brotherhood. He struggled to achieve the noble ideals of justice, equality and freedom in order to contribute to the cause of social reconstruction. He was one of the greatest political thinkers that India produced in the twentieth century. From Marxism to Socialism, from Socialism to *Sarvodaya* and finally to 'Total Revolution' has been the journey of his thought and action. Very often his views on specific national and international issues aroused sharp reactions and criticisms but his integrity and sincerity was never in doubt.

Jayaprakash Narayan was born on 11 October, 1902, in a village namely Sitabdiara in Bihar. He was the fourth child of his parents. His political career began as a nationalist. Freedom and responsibility remained the basic impulses of his life. He said, "Feedom became one of the beacon lights of my life, and it has remained so ever since. Freedom, with the passing of years transcended the mere freedom of country and embraced freedom of man everywhere and from every sort of trammel, above all, it meant freedom of the human personality, freedom of the mind, freedom of the spirit. The freedom has become passion of life and I shall not see it compromised for bread, for power, for security, for prosperity, for the glory of the State or for anything else."[1] He passed matriculation examination in 1919. He came in contact with revolutionary leaders. The simplicity of Gandhiji had a profound impact on him. Gopala Krishna Gokhale was the first influence on him.

Jayaprakash Narayan was married to Prabhavati Devi in 1920. Gandhiji started the non-co-operation movement. He asked the students to boycott all educational institutions run by the British Government. Jayaprakash Narayan left the college and joined the movement. He said, "As a boy, like most boys of those days, I was an ardent nationalist and leaned towards the revolutionary cult of which Bengal was the noble leader at that time. But even then the story of the South African *Satyagraha* had fascinated my young heart. Before my revolutionary leanings could mature, Gandhiji's first non-co-operation movement swept over the land as a strangely uplifting hurricane. I, too, was one of the thousands of young men of those days, who, like leaves in the storm, were swept away and momentarily lifted up to the skies".[2] After passing the intermediate examination, he went to U.S.A. for higher education. He lieved in San Francisco for seven years. He studied at the Universities of California, Iowa, Wisconsin and Ohio. He took his Master's degree in Sociology from Ohio University. For want of money, he had to work in the fields, factories and hotels to meet his expenses.

One of his friends, Avrom Landy introduced Jayaprakash Narayan to *Marxism*. He read almost everything that Marx had written. He said, "It was in land of resilent and successful capitalism, in the United States of America . . . that I became a convert to Marxism, or precisely, to Soviet Communism as it was then. It was at Madison, Wisconsin the home of La-Follete progressivism then, that in the company of Jewish and European born fellow students I drank deep at the fountain of Marxism. I think we left nothing unread of Marxism that was available in the English language then and with the help of a brilliant student of German even read some of the untranslated Marxism classics."[3] The writings of M.N. Roy made an impact on his political mind. He read the writings of M.N. Roy. He made his acquaintance with him. He said, "Naturally, he had a great hand in moulding my thought and leading me to Communism, which was still a revolutionary doctrine. That Roy was a colleague of Lenin and was a big personality in the Communist International, made him in my young eyes a hero and a great Indian . . . In the States I was drawn towards him as a disciple to the master".[4] The impact of M.N. Roy converted him into a confirmed Marxist.

Jayaprakash Narayan left the United States for India in September 1929. During this time Gandhiji was preparing for the next phase of struggle for independence. Jayaprakash Narayan went to Wardha to see Gandhiji. He attended the Lahore Session of the Indian National Congress in 1929. He was impressed by Nehru. Nehru invited him to Allahabad to lead the Labour Research Department of the Indian National Congress. He stayed at Allahabad with Nehru and his relations with him became very close. He did not join the Communist Party in India. He never became a complete apologist for Russian Communism. He wanted to establish a separate Communist Party. In 1932 the second disobedience campaign was started. He became the acting General-Secretary of the Congress. He was arrested in Madras on 7 September, 1932 and was sent to Nasik Jail. In jail, he came in contact with some Congress leaders. They prepared a blue print of a socialist party to be organised with the Congress. He was the main architect of the Congress Socialist Party. He was elected Organising Secretary of the newly formed party. He propagated the socialist ideas on Marxist line. He urged the people to develop a mass movement consisting of the working classes and the peasants. In the formative period of the Congress Socialist Party, he played a pioneering role and left his stamp on the character of the party. He was in favour of creating a broad socialist front to fight against imperialism.

Jayaprakash Narayan published an English Weekly called *Congress Socialist,* from Bombay in 1939. He organised the Kisan and Mazdoor bodies to propagate the *socialism.* He organised a 'Youth Society', a 'Women's Society' and a 'Self-Help Society'. He opposed the World War II. He was arrested in 1940 and imprisoned for nine months. In jail, he kept on writing articles. To quote Gandhiji, "The arrest of Sri Jayaprakash Narayan is unfortunate. He is no ordinary worker. He is an authority on socialism. It may be said that what he does not know of western socialism nobody else in India does. He is a fine fighter. He has forsaken all for the sake of the deliverence of his country. His industry is tireless. His capacity for suffering is not to be excelled."[5] He kept up his political activities in jail through political discussion and debates. In 1942, he escaped from Hazaribagh Central Jail. He started an underground movement and trained a guerrilla brigade. In 1944, he himself acknowledged that he did not believe in non-violence. He left for Nepal and organised an 'Azad Dasta' there. He was arrested in September 1943. He was released from the jail in 1946. In July 1946, he visited Lahore and believed that the time was ripe for a revolution.

Jayaprakash Narayan advocated for the adoption of the peaceful and democratic path to establish socialism in India in 1947. In 1948, he emphasized on the purity of means and denounced the power politics. In 1950, he advocated the creation of a society of free and equal peoples, a society based on certain values of human and social life, values, which could never be sacrificed in the name of theory or the party line or expedience of any sort. There was a profound transformation in the political and moral make up of Jayaprakash Narayan after Gandhiji's death. In 1952, he attempted to create a joint platform for all democratic and socialist parties in opposition to Congress. In June 1952, he negotiated a merger between the KMPP and Socialist Party and thus was born the Praja Socialist Party (PSP). In February 1953, Nehru invited him to join the Government along with some of his co-workers. Jayaprakash Narayan suggested a 14-Point Minimum Programme, which might constitute a concrete ground for the Congress-PSP agreement. Nehru expressed his inability to implement these reforms. In 1951, he recommended a serious study of the *Sarvodaya* plan, for economic development.

Jayaprakash Narayan emphasized on the postulate goodness of the individual for a good society. He advocated a path beyond *materialism* to find the incentives for goodness. Thus, he abandoned Dialectical Materialism and adopted Gandhism. He strongly recommended peaceful means for establishing a socialist society. He said, "Both Socialism and Communism are faced with failures. Communism . . . has ended up in State Capitalism and dictatorship . . . Socialism, . . . has become only a parliamentary or legalistic creed. Thus, both the methods of violence and of parliamentary action have failed. *Gandhism,* to my mind, offers the third action."[6] In 1954, he declared to dedicate his life to the Bhoodan Movement. He became a *Jeevandani.* He retired from active party politics. He established a Sarvodaya Ashram in 1956. In 1957, he gave up even the basic membership of the PSP. He said, "The politics of *Sarvodaya* can have no party and no concern with power. Rather, its aim will be to see that all centres of power are established. The more this new politics grows, the more the old politics shrinks. A real withering away of the State."[7] In April 1958, he went to Europe. He returned to India in September 1958. After his return, he voiced his conviction that the only way to move the people was to awaken to go back to Gandhiji to him, Sarvodaya was a higher and truer form of democratic socialism.

In 1959, Jayaprakash Narayan advocated for the adoption of a decentralised socio-political order in India. In 1961, he stressed the need and urgency of direct participation of the people in the management of their affairs as for as possible. He advocated the Panchayati Raj. In 1970, he expressed the view that the whole social system should be decentralised and reconstructed on the basis of communitarian society and Panchayati Raj. In 1971, he employed his efforts to solve the dacoits problem of the Chambal valley. On 15 April, 1973, his wife died. He had lost interest in life after his wife death. In 1974 he gave the idea of Total Revolution. From 1954 to 1971, he played an active role in the Sarvodaya movement. In 1975, he demanded the resignation of Mrs. Indira Gandhi from Prime Ministership in compliance with the High Court Judgement. Emergency was declared on 26 June, 1975 and he was arrested and later released on 12 November, 1975. In jail, he fell seriously ill. His health deteriorated further. At last, he died in his sleep on 8 October, 1979.

Among the works of Jayaprakash Narayan are a number of books and booklets throwing light on his socio-economic philosophy. These include *Why socialism, Towards struggle, In the Lahore Fort, A plea for the Reconstruction of Indian Polity, From Socialism to Sarvodaya and Swaraj for the People.*

Jayaprakash Narayan was initiated in the Marxist philosophy during his student days in America. He read Marx's *Das Kapital* and M.N. Roy's pamphlets. To quote Ajit Bahattacharjee, "The overall impact, in a period in which no positive moves towards independence were being made in India, was overwhelming. Marxism seemed to provide not only the key to independence, but to social equality and even personal liberty in those holydam days."[8] Jayaprakash Narayan did not approve the type of the communist state established in Russia. Ajit Bhattacharjee said, "Fascism he had rejected much earlier, but the experience of Soviet Russia showed him that irrespective of the ideals inspiring communism, a strong state apparatus that treated all opposition as treason, led to dictatorship and tyranny, not freedom in any sense."[9]

Jayaprakash Narayan had faith in Marxism as far as the ends are concerned but for the means to achieve them he had a conviction for the Gandhian approach. He was for the abolition of private ownership of land, socialisation of industries, reduction in disparities of income and wealth, social equality, cooperative and collective farming and community initiative through institutions like village panchayats. He said, "Socialism is not merely anti-capitalism nor statism. Nationalisa-tion of industry and collectivisation of agriculture are important aspects of socialist economy; but in themselves they are not socialism. Under socialism there is no exploitation of man by man, no injustice and oppression, no insecurity and an equitable distribution of wealth, and services and opportunities. Even in a nationalised and collectivised economy there may be exploitation, injustice, oppression, insecurity and glaring inequalities. If under such an economy, all political and economic power is concentrated in the hands of a party oligarchy there can be no socialism but its suppression, no revolution but reaction."[10]

Jayaprakash Narayan had his differences with the concept of socialism evolved by Nehru. He said, "A natural outcome of centralisation of power and administration is bureaucracy. The central executive or cabinet is so over-burdened with work that it is compelled to leave more and more to, and depend more and more upon, the permanent officials, who in course of time gather more and more power for themselves. This soon leads to a dangerous autocracy, the autocracy of the bureaucrats, which is difficult to fight because it works in the shadows and is hard to get at."[11] According to his concept of a socialist state the initiative for social change should come from the people themselves and power should flow from bottom to the top. The state should only provide the legislative support for it. It should also play its role in the matter of nationalisation of industries and supply of credit and other facilities to the cottage and small-scale industries.

REFERENCES

1. *Jayaprakash Narayan: from Socialism to Sarvodaya,* Akhil Bharat Sarva Seva Sangh Prakashan, Kashi, 1959, pp. 9-10.
2. *Ibid.*, p. 10
3. *Ibid.*
4. Jayaprakash Narayan on M.N. Roy, *The Radical Humanist,* Vol. 41, No. 12, March, 1978, p. 8.
5. *Harijan,* 16-3-1940.
6. *Jayaprakash Narayan: Socialism, Sarvodaya and Democracy,* Asia Publishing House, Bombay, 1964, p. 120.
7. *Ibid.*, pp. 170-71.
8. Ajit Bhattacharjee, *Jayaprakash Narayan—A Political Biography,* Vikas Publication House, New Delhi, 1979, p. 47.
9. *Ibid.*, p. 4.
10. *Jayaprakash Narayan: Democratic Socialism and Sarvodaya,* Youth Education Publication, Kirki, 1975, p. 159.
11. *Ibid.*, p. 160.

2

JAYAPRAKASH NARAYAN ON SOCIALISM

Jayaprakash Narayan was an ardent Marxist in his early phase of political career. He began by analysing the Indian society from the Marxian viewpoint. He came to the conclusion that the reason of povertv of the Indian masses was not merely the foreign economic exploitation but Indian bourgeois class also played significant role in exploiting the natives. He believed in scientific socialism and its evolutionary nature. To him, socialism was the common ownership of the means of production and distribution and equal opportunities to all the people. He agreed in the beginning to bring socialism by the power of the State.

Jayaprakash Narayan agreed that without political independence the socialistic programme could not be implemented. He placed a great emphasis on agricultural development of the country. He suggested cooperative farming. To balance the economy of the country, he favoured setting up of industries owned by State as well as community. He suggested an agro-industrial economy as the solution for India and its development. He gave a lot of importance to planning in the economic development.

In his later stage, Jayaprakash Narayan renounced Marxism. He came to the conclusion that Marxian socialism was not the remedy for the problems of humanity in general. He realised, socialism tended to culminate into state capitalism. He grew into vehement critiques of the Russian totalitarianism and statism. His ideologies and thought went beyond communism. In the post-independence period, he joined the Sarvodaya movement.

Jayaprakash Narayan agreed that the main problem was not that of production but of centralisation. He advocated decentralisation. He proposed to organise the political and economic system independent of the state interference. He visualised the pyramidal structure of the political and economic system. He agreed on co-operative agriculture. He was critical of the Second Five-Year Plan.

Jayaprakash Narayan never took the directives from the World Communist Movement. He came to India as a confirmed Marxist, but did not join the communist movement in India. He joined the Indian National Congress straightaway. He was a great propounder of Indian socialism. To him, socialist movement in India was a part of the national freedom struggle. The association of the socialist movement with freedom struggle had an important consequence. Nationalism, which might in theory be regarded as a departure from socialist internationalism, in practice, helped the socialists to escape from the embrace of the communists. It was on this issue of subordination to Moscow that they parted company, said Jayaprakash Narayan. He advocated democratic socialism and Gandhian spiritual means to establish it. To him, there was no dichotomy between socialism and the Indian culture.

Jayaprakash Narayan considered socialism as a complete theory of socio-economic reconstruction. To him socialism was a theory and technique of widespread planning. Its objective was harmonious and well balanced growth of the whole society. In between 1929 and 1946 he was an ardent believer in Marxian socialism. He regarded socialism as an economic principle. The aim of socialism should be to eradicate the economic inequality and concentration of wealth in a few hands. He said, "It is a society, in which all are workers—a classless society. It is a society, in which human labour is not subject to exploitation with interest of private property, in which all wealth is truly national—in which there are no unearned incomes and no large economic disparities, in which human life and progress are planned and where all live for all".[1]

Jayaprakash Narayan believed in the principle of dialectical materialism. He said, social division is an organic process of society. Marx showed that its primary source lay in the manner, in which men earned their livelihood.[2] To him, Marxian dialectical materialism provided the basis of a socialist's inquiry into the causes of inequality. He analysed the class organisation in Indian society. He believed that Indian bourgeois could not lead the anti-imperialist movement. They had always been in league and compromise with the British imperialism. He stood for social and economic equality.

Jayaprakash Narayan outlined the following 15-Point Programme of the All India Congress Socialist Party in 1934. They are:

(1) Transfer of all power to the Producing masses.
(2) Development of the economic life of the country to be planned and controlled by the state.
(3) Socialisation of key and principal industries with a view to the progressive socialisation of all the instruments of production, distribution and exchange.
(4) State monopoly of foreign trade.
(5) Organisation of cooperatives for production, distribution and credit in the unsocialised sector of economic life.
(6) Elimination of princes and landlords and all other classes of exploiters without compensation.
(7) Redistribution of land to peasants.
(8) Encouragement and promotion of co-operative and collective farming by the state.
(9) Liquidation of debts owed by peasants and workers.
(10) Recognition of the right to work or maintenance by the state.
(11) To everyone according to his needs and from everyone according to his capacity to be the basis ultimately of distribution and production of economic goods.
(12) Adult franchise on a functional basis.
(13) No support to or discrimination between religions by the state and no recognition of any distinction based on caste or community.
(14) No discrimination between the sexes by the state.
(15) Repudiation of the so-called public Debt of India.'[3]

Jayaprakash Narayan stood for the reduction of land revenue, the limitation of consumption expenditure and the nationalisation of industries. Since 1934, he believed that socialism alone could be the basis of freedom of India. In 1940, he advocated collective ownership and control of all large scale production. He urged that the State should nationalise heavy transport, shipping, mining and the heavy industries. He observed, "The law of the land will be based on the will of the people freely expressed by them. The ultimate basis of mainte-nance of order shall be the sanction and concurrence of the people.

"The free Indian state shall guarantee full individual and civil liberty and cultural and religious freedom, provided that there shall be no freedom, overthrown by violence the constitution framed by the Indian people through a Constituent Assembly."
"The state shall not discriminate in any manner between citizens

of the nation. Every citizen shall be guaranteed equal rights. All distinctions of birth and privilege shall be abolished. There shall be no titles emanating whether from inherited social status or the state."

"The political and economic organisation of the state shall be based on principles of social justice and economic freedom. While this organisation shall conduce to the satisfaction of the national require-ments of every member of society, material satisfaction shall not be its sole objective. It shall aim at healthy living and the moral and intellectual development of the individual. To this end to secure social justice, the state shall endeavour to promote small-scale production carried on by individual or co-operative effort for the equal benefit of all concerned. All large-scale collective production shall be eventually brought under collective ownership and control, and in this behalf the *State* shall begin by nationalising heavy transport, shipping, mining and the heavy industries. The textile industry shall be progressively decentralised."

"The life of the village shall be reorganised and the villages shall be made self-governing units, self-sufficient in as large a measure as possible. The land laws of the country shall be drastically reformed on the principle that land shall belong to the actual cultivator alone and that no cultivator shall have more land than is necessary to support his family on a fair standard of living. This will end the various systems of landlordism on the one hand and firm bondage on the other."

"The state shall protect the interests of the classes, but when these imprige upon the interests of those who have been poor and downtrodden it shall defend the latter and thus restore the balance of social justice."

"In all state-owned and state-managed enterprises, the workers shall be represented in the management through their elected representa-tives and shall have an equal share in it with the representatives of the Government."

"In the Indian states, there shall be complete democratic government established and in accordance with the principles of abolition of social distinction and equality between citizens, there shall not be any titular heads of the states in the persons of Rajas and Nawabs."

"This is the order, which the Congress envisages and which it shall work to establish. The Congress firmly believes that this order shall bring happiness, prosperity and freedom to the people of all races and religions in India, who together shall build on these foundations a great and glorious nation."[4]

Jayaprakash Narayan stood for village reorganisation. He suggested that land should belong to the actual cultivator. He said, "The only solution is to clear away all the vested interests that lead in any manner whatever to the exploitation of the tiller of the soil, liquidate all agrarian debts; pool the holdings and collective farming, state and co-operative credit and marketing system and co-operative subsidiary industries."[5] Cooperative efforts and planning only could provide the balance between agriculture and industry.

In August 1946, Jayaprakash Narayan formulated a thirteen-point constructive work programme to establish Gram Raj. They are:'

(1) Enrolment of Congress members. Attempts should be made to enrol every adult villager. Meetings of the enrolled members should be held.
(2) A cultural centre should be opened where newspapers should be read and such other activities conducted as adult literacy, dramatics, folk songs, study circles, library, posters, agricultural advice, etc.
(3) Sevadal and Akhada work.
(4) Problems of sanitation, roads, bunds, etc. tackled in a practical way. Collective labour for common purposes should be encouraged.
(5) Untouchability work.
(6) Communal harmony work.
(7) Prohibition.
(8) Survey of conditions.
(9) Redress of grievances.
(10) Founding of Grain Banks.
(11) Propaganda in neighbouring villages.
(12) Co-operative marketing.
(13) Work among women and children'.[6]

Jayaprakash Narayan suggested that the state should set up its own industries. He also suggested municipal or community ownership of industries. He observed, "I advocate development of these co-operatives and community owned industries; firstly, because I do not believe it possible to find employment for many years to come for our surplus population, which would swell further, at least, by twenty per cent by the revolution in agriculture, in large industry alone; secondly, because I desire to prevent the state from acquiring the sole-monopoly in industry and employment. The state, under socialism threatens, as in Russia, far from withering away, to become an all-powerful tyrant maintaining a stranglehold over the entire body of citizens. This leads to totalitarianism of the type we witness in Russia to-day."[7]

Jayaprakash Narayan in the mean time realised that democracy was essential for socialism. He said, "There can be no socialism without democracy. It is a common mistake these days to think that there must be the dictatorship of the proletariat in a socialist state. This is against the teaching of Marx. The dictatorship of the proletariat has a place only in the transitional period capitalism to socialism. And in this period too it is not inevitable in every case."[8]

Jayaprakash Narayan described his concept of socialism as an economic and political democracy. In this democracy man will neither be slave to capital nor to a party or the state. Man will be free. He will have to serve society, which will provide him with employment and the means of livelihood, but within limits he will be free to choose his avocation and station in life. He will be free to express his opinions and there will be opportunities for him to rise to his full moral stature. There will be no great difference between man and man—except the difference of physical and mental endownments—for there will be no great difference in incomes. He pointed out, "violent revolution and dictatorship might conceivably lead to a socialist democray; but in the only country (USSR) where it has been tried, it has led to something very different, that is, to a bureaucratic state, in which democracy does not exist. I should like to take a lesson from history."[9]

Jayaprakash Narayan emphasized on ethical values and good means to achieve socialism. He said, "There were many things the Mahatma Gandhi taught us. But the greatest thing he taught us was that means are ends, that evil means can never lead to good ends and that fair ends require fair means. Some of us may have been sceptical of this truth but recent world events and events at home have convinced me that nothing, but good means will enable us to reach the goal of a good society, which is socialism".[10] He believed that greater the freedom, higher would be the level of socialism. He said, "Democratic socialism must become our life's mission, the philosophy of our life. We must accept democracy and all that it stands for, for thus alone can we reach the goal of socialism. Democratic socialism involves acceptance of democratic means, peaceful methods and constructive approach, in the attainment of our goal."[11]

Jayaprakash Narayan emphasised on democratic means to be followed under the then existing conditions of the country. He stated that Marxism was itself a confluence of three streams of ideas, that is, classical economics of Britain, revolutionary socialism of France and Philosophy of Germany. He pleaded to combine the Marxian thought with the thought and practice of Gandhi and achieve a synthesis of their own. He came closer to Gandhi and pleaded for ethical politics since 1948. He stood firmly for Gandhism by 1952. He said, "For many years I have worshipped at the shrine of the Goddess of Dialectical Materialism, which seemed to me intellectually more satisfying than any other philosophy. But while the main quest of philosophy remains unsatisfied, it has become patent to me, that materiaism of any sort robs man of the means to become truly human. In a material civilisation man has no rational incentive to be good. It may be that in the kingdom of dialectical materialism fear makes men conform and the party takes the place of God. But when that God himself turns vicious, to be vicious becomes a universal code."[12]

In 1951, Jayaprakash Narayan declared that *Sarvodaya* was not a crankish creed, but it was the first attempt to establish a new social order—a classless and casteless society. He said, 'Some years back it became clear to me that socialism as it is understood it today. cannot take mankind to the subline goals of freedom, equality, brotherhood and peace . . . unless socialism is transformed into Sarvodaya, those goals would remain beyond its reach."[13] He expounded the contents of Sarvodaya Plan and suggested to the Congress to accept and implement it. He stated that Bhoodan was the first step towards a total revolution.

Jayaprakash Narayan advocated Gandhi's path of peace and love to achieve socialism. He believed in Gandhian method of internal change in man. He advised the people to follow simplicity in their life. According to him, state cannot force the individual to live according to this ideal. Only the Gandhian and Sarvodaya principles showed the way of sharing of wealth, which was the real and full socialism. He said, "Socialism for me was always a way of life. It represented a set of values, to which we owed allegiance voluntary and which we tried to put into practice in our lives. These values we did not see developing any where as a result of merely institutional changes, whether economic or political."[14] In 1957, he advocated people's socialism. He realised that representative government was not enough. His aim was to create a classless, stateless and partyless society. He visualised a chain of communities. All the communities from bottom to top would be organically inter-related and independent in their spheres.

To Jayaprakash Narayan, political decentralisation cannot be effective without economic decentralisation. In the communitarian society, the role of the state would be minimum. The state should regulate and legislate for the formation of a Panchayati Raj. He maintained that in the communitarian society, the people's socialism could be achieved.

Jayaprakash Narayan advocated the philosophy of Total Revolution since 1974. He was influenced by the teachings of Gandhi, Vinoba, M.N. Roy and Lenin to a certain extent. To him, the ideal of Total Revolution was similar to Gandhi's ideal of Purna Swaraj. He said, "Any Gandhian approach or model is one of a continuous revolution which I have called Total Revolution. Satyagraha or non-violent struggle is the essence of this revolution. It is also dialectical in a special sense—it makes a struggle between Individual and Society, Authority and Freedom, Elite and the Masses, Property and Non-possession, Labour and Capital and so on."[15]

Jayaprakash Narayan advocated a seven-fold scheme of revolutions. He said, "I have been saying that total revolution is a combination of seven revolutions—social, economic, political, cultural, ideological or intellectual, educational and spiritual. This number may be increased or decreased. For instance, the cultural revolution may include educational and ideological revolution . . . Similarly, intellectual revolution may be split up into two—scientific and philosophical. Even spiritual revolution can be viewed as made up of the moral and spiritual or it can be looked upon part of the cultural. And so on."[16] To him, the Total Revolution would bring revolution in all aspects of society as well as the individual simultaneously. It would change the entire system. It aims at renunciation of the lust of power. He said, "In a democracy the people do have the right to ask for the resignation of an elected government if it has gone corrupt and has been misruling. And if there is a legislature that persists in supporting such a government it too must go so that the people might choose better representatives."[17]

Jayaprakash Narayan visualised a radical change in the ownership of the means of production. He laid emphasis on agricultural development, equitable land ownership, the application of appropriate technology to agriculture, the development of domestic and rural industries and the widest possible expansion of small industries, regional planning and development. In this scheme he had given importance to individual.

REFERENCES

1. S.A. Ansari, *Socialist Movement in India: The Radical Humanist,* Vol. XXXI, No. 49, December 24, 1967, p. 577.
2. Jayaprakash Narayan, *Why Socialism?* The All-India Congress Socialist Party, Banaras, 1936, p. 1.
3. *Ibid.,* pp. 28-29.
4. Jayaprakash Narayan, *Towards Struggle,* Padma Publications, Bombay, 1946, p. 78.
5. *Ibid.,* p. 90.
6. Brahmanand, *Communitarian Society and Panchayat Raj,* Navachetna Prakashan, Varanasi, 1970, p. 49.
7. Jayaprakash Narayan, *My Picture of Socialism,* 1946, p. 5.
8. *Ibid.*
9. *Ibid.,* pp. 49-56.
10. Report of the Sixth Annual Conference held at Nasik, March 19 to 21, 1948, Socialist Party, Bombay, p. 96.
11. *Ibid.*
12. Jayaprakash Narayan, *A Picture of Sarvodaya Social Order,* A Sarvodaya Publication, Tanjore, 1961, p. 18.
13. Jayaprakash Narayan, *Towards a New Society,* The Congress for Cultural Freedom, New Delhi, 1958, p. 21.
14. Jayaprakash Narayan, *Gandhi, Vinoba and Bhoodan Movement,* Colefore, England, (Address given before United Nations Association).
15. J.D. Sethi, *Gandhi Today,* Vikas Publishing House, New Delhi, 1978, pp. ix-x.
16. Jayaprakash Narayan, *Towards Total Revolution,* Popular Prakashan, Bombay, 1978, pp. 87-88.
17. Jayaprakash Narayan, *From Behind the Bars in Independent India,* Samajwadi Yuva Samaj Jansabha, Calcutta, 1976, p. 172.

3

JAYAPRAKASH NARAYAN ON INDIVIDUAL AND STATE

Jayaprakash Narayan laid emphasis on individual dignity, initiative and *liberty*. He gave the central place to the individual in his political philosophy and criticized the political, economic and social systems. For him individual was an end and all the other association and organisations were the means. Man was moral and good by nature. He tried to infuse the spirit of self-reliance in the individual. He was the champion of individual freedom. Freedom was an essential aspect of human nature and the basic human value to him. His entire philosophy was concerned with satisfying the man's urge for freedom. Without freedom, man was not a human being in real sense.

Jayaprakash Narayan was an individualist as well as a socialist. He held that man should sacrifice his interests for the sake of society. To him, social interest was higher than individual interest. He believed that the good of the individual could be best obtained by subordinating his interest to the higher interest of the community. He laid stress on leading a severe self-disciplined simple life. His approach to the individual was spiritual. He said that whatever the nature of human spirit may be, it definitely seems to be of a higher order than the Mind. He was of the opinion that reason alone would not enable man to shape a better future for himself. He agreed with Vinoba's statement that the Age of Reason and Politics is over and a new Age of Spirituality and *Science* has dawned.

Jayaprakash Narayan gave more significance to the individual and his status, from the beginning of his political life. He said, "Individualism has been the prominent motif in our culture only in the sense that the perfection of the individual has been its deal; never in the sense of narrow, self-seeking individualism, which is the motive in capitalist society. And if individual perfection is the goal, the socialist has not the least difficulty in showing that such perfection can come about only by aiming at the utmost common good".[1] He did not think the individual as an end in himself. He gave importance to the society. To him, the society, the social environment and the economic forces were more important. He considered the individual to be of little importance in the context of the social whole.

Jayaprakash Narayan came to realise the importance of the individual as an end in himself, in the later phase of his political career. He declared that man was not just a heap of matter. Man is an ethical being. He said, "Human nature, apart from the instincts of self and race preservation, is most likely of a neutral character which acquires moral tones in accordance with social conditioning".[2] He recommended spiritual approach because it elevates the individual to a moral plane, and urges him, without reference to any objective outside of himself, to endeavour to realise his own true nature and fulfil the purpose of his being. This endeavour becomes the powerful motive force that drives him in its natural course to the good and the true. It will be seen as an important corollary of this that only when materialism is transcended does individual man come into his own and become an end in himself.

Jayaprakash Narayan believed in the change of art. His approach to man was spiritual. He believed in human values. He believed in training of man to make him good inspired by some ethical values. He said, "I feel convinced, therefore, that man must go beyond the material to find the incentive to goodness. As a corollary, I feel further that the task of social reconstruction cannot succeed under the inspiration of a materialist philosophy".[3] To him, science, and spirituality complement each other and need one another. He said, "The more he identifies himself with larger and larger numbers of people the more spiritually advanced he is. He wants to identify himself with his family . . . he identifies himself. . . he may identify himself with his state, may be with his nation, with his country and ultimately with the whole world. This is spiritual realisation".[4]

For a good society, the constituent individuals should also be good. Jayaprakash Narayan remarked that social reconstruction is impossible without human reconstruction. Society cannot be good unless individual men are good, and particularly those men who form the elite of society. He believed that a new man was necessary for the success of democracy. He placed the individual in the central position. He fully believed in man's worth and dignity, and in his rights and responsibilities. To him in Sarvodaya society, all the powers of administration and construction would be in the hands of people.

Jayaprakash Narayan believed in transferring all the powers to the people at large and not to a few who claim to exercise power on behalf of the people, in his total revolution phase. He believed in changing the entire system—political, economic, social, etc. as well as individual, intellectual, cultural, moral or spiritual. Without a change in the individual, there would not be a total revolution. He placed equal stress on human as well as social aspects for the reconstruction of a new society. He wanted to change human values through a social revolution.

Jayaprakash Narayan was a champion of individual freedom. Man should be free to develop his personality. Everyone should have equal opportunity for one's all round development. He said, "Freedom became one of the beacon-lights of my life and it has remained so ever since. Freedom with the passing of the years, transcended the mere freedom of man everywhere and from very sort of trammel—above all it meant the freedom of the human personality, freedom of the mind, freedom of the spirit".[5] Freedom should include freedom from exploita-tion, from hunger, from poverty. To him, man without freedom is not a human being. He remarked that a society which denies man, his freedom in truth denies his humanity, because if the freedom of the spirit is taken away then man becomes only an animal.

Jayaprakash Narayan rejected the theory of the dictatorship of the proletariat only because there was no democratic freedom envisaged. He was of the opinion that the people's instinct is always in favour of freedom and democracy and it is never natural for them deliberately to subjects themselves to a dictatorship. He criticized the Parliamentary system of government and the party system. To him, totalitarianism was a crime against man. Man by nature should work for freedom. His philosophy of total revolution is deeply committed to resuscitate the rights and liberties of the individuals.

To Jayaprakash Narayan, the state was a means to an end. He criticized the totalitarian state of Soviety Russia. He advocated the diffusion of power to the lowest level. He was critical of the welfare state because he was in favour of giving the least responsibilities to the state. He was critical of the nation state and was for a World state. He did not care about the origin of the state. He was mainly concerned with the state as it was in existence. He believed in a stateless society.

Jayaprakash Narayan's views about state evolved with his career and thought process. He maintained that no party in the world of today can build up socialism unless it has the machinery of the state in its hands. State also appeared as a coercive power to him. In the pre-independence period, he appreciated considerably the achievement of the Soviet State. He said, "when the state is in your hands, you can legislate, you can use the whole magnificent apparatus of propaganda and education that, modern science has made available; you can enforce your will. And if there is resistance, you can use the coercive arm of the state—the police and army to crush it. Behind every piece of legislation lies the state's power to persuade and ultimately, to coerce".[6]

In the post-independence period, Jayaprakash Narayan seemed to have lost all sympathy for totalitarian state of Soviet Union. In 1948, he remarked, "The experience of the totalitarian countries, whether, Fascist or Communist has shown that if the state is looked upon as the sole agent of social reconstruction, we get nothing but a regimented society in which the state is all powerful and popular initiative is extinct and the individual is made a cog in the vast unhappy machine".[7] He came to realise that ideal of stateless society was not achievable. He emphasised on communitarian society. He advocated setting up of co-operatives and community owned industries to avoid totalitarianism. He said, "I desire to prevent the state from acquiring the sole monopoly in industry and employment. The state under socialism threatens, as in Russia, far from withering away, to become an all-powerful tyrant maintaining a stranglehold over the entire body of citizens. This leads to totalitarianism of the type we witness in Russia."[8]

Jayaprakash Narayan pleaded for the decentralisation. He felt the need of a fully democratic state in India and opposed the idea of dictatorship of the proletariat. He said, "The state in socialist India must be a fully democratic state. It is a common mistake these days to think that there must be the dictatorship of the proletariat in a socialist state. This is against the teachings of Marx. The dictatorship of proletariat has a place only in the transitional period from capitalism to socialism."[9] He was critical of the principle of absolute sovereignty of the state. He conceived the idea of a state without any political party. He suggested the abolition of party system.

Jayaprakash Narayan believed in the withering away of the state. He pleaded for devolution of power to the maximum extent. He said, 'As questioning about politics were not confined to party system alone, fundamental questions arose in my mind as to the place and role of the state in human society, particularly in relation to the goals of social life that had fixed themselves before me. Perhaps, my schooling in Marxism with its ideals of a stateless society, made these questions more pointed and troublesome. Though I had given up the basic postulates of Marxism. . . . I continued to feel strongly that human could be fully and wholly realised only in a stateless society. I was, and am, not sure if the state would ever wither away completely. But I am sure that it is one of the noblest goals of social endeavour to ensure that the powers and functions and spheres of the state are reduced as far as possible. I became at this time, and still am, an ardent believer, like Gandhi, in the maxim that that government was the best that governed the least."[10]

Jayaprakash Narayan wished to organise the social order in such a manner in which the power of the state were to be diffused into smaller units of communitarian centres. He believed that the smaller units of power would enable the individual to play a greater part. He was totally against the monistic state. He said that the intermediate associations between the individual and the state should be purposely and deliberately created so that freedom might not be nominal but real, and democracy might not be only government by consent but also by direct participation. The state was only a part of society. His ideal was Panchayat Raj. To him the state should regulate and legislate for the formation of a Panchayat Raj; but the day-to-day working should be outside the purview of the State Government.

Jayaprakash Narayan believed that in the name of welfare the state had assumed larger powers and responsibilities. He said, "In the present world the state not only in its totalitarian form but also in its welfare variety is assuming larger and larger powers and responsibilities. The welfare state, in the name of welfare, threatens as much to enslave man to the state as the totalitarian".[11] He criticized the nation state. He gave the concept of a world community. He was a nationalist but did not believe in aggressive version of nationalism. To him, the world community only could do justice to the suppressed sections of Asian and African humanity. In the final phase of his political life, he advocated for peoples Government from below against the totalitarian state. He laid stress on the devolution of power reaching to the lowest level. His concept of state remained fluid and shifting in consonance to his phases of political evolution. He conceded that a fully stateless society was beyond the reach of men.

Jayaprakash Narayan rejected the violent and insurrectionary method and stressed on peaceful moral means. To him, revolution meant an all-round change in all aspects of man as well as his institutions. He favoured gradual replacement of the old order by the new social order to bring about a social revolution. Revolution was a long term process of social change and not an event to him. He regarded revolution a means and not as end in itself. He advocated revolution by consent. He believed in the persuasion and education of the individuals for social change.

In the beginning Jayaprakash Narayan believed in proletarian revolution and the concept of class struggle. To him, Parliamentary democracy was not likely to be much effective. He advocated openly to adopt violent means for achieving the independence. He urged the people to develop a mass movement against the British Government. Throughout the colonial period, he often advocated the use of arms in the struggle for freedom. In 1944, he acknowledged that he was not a believer in non-violence. During the post-independence period, he advocated the need for adopting democratic means. The death of Gandhiji and the riots of the partition further convinced him of the futility of violent means. He accepted the Gandhian technique of non-violent methods. He said, "There were many things that Mahatma Gandhi taught us. But the greatest thing he taught us was that evil means can never lead to good ends. Some of us may have been sceptical of this truth but recent world events and events at home convinced me that nothing but good means will enable us to reach the goal of a good society, which is socialism."[12]

According to Jayaprakash Narayan, five kinds of activities were comprised within the term democratic method. These were organisation, propaganda, agitation, struggle and constructive work. He criticised the violent means as counter-revolutionary. In 1957, he said, "If theory of violence as a midwife of revolution was not challenged in its entirety, at least, this much became clear to me (a) that in a society where it was possible for the people by democratic means to bring about social change it would be counter-revolutionary to resort to violence and (b) that socialism could not exist, not to be created, in the absence of the democratic freedoms."[13]

During the Gandhian and Sarvodaya phase of his political life, Jayaprakash Narayan stressed adoption of democratic and non-violent moral means for social revolution. The social revolution would bring about an all-round change in all aspects of human life. He said, "A social revolution is a fundamental change in the economic political and social power structure, so that power comes to be exercised at the workplace. This implies fundamental change in property relationships, in respect of ownership management and disposal of profits. It implies end of exploitation, employer-employee relationships and socio-economic inequality. This also implies universal freedom and a radically different set of values governing individual and social lives".[14] The purpose of total revolution was both internal and external change.

Jayaprakash Narayan believed that social revolution could be brought about neither by constitutional means nor by violent means. It could be brought only by non-violent means. Non-violent social revolution would be brought about directly by the people. The methods would be persuasion and conversion. He stressed on social revolution through human revolution. During the total revolution phase, he advocated Gandhian non-violent militancy to attain permanent social change. He laid emphasis on voluntary mass action for bringing about a revolutionary change. His technique of revolution was neither violent nor completely non-violent. It was a practical method of peaceful mass action.

REFERENCES

1. Jayaprakash Narayan, *Socialism, Sarvodaya and Democracy*, Asia Publishing House, Bombay, 1964, pp. 15-16.
2. Jayaprakash Narayan, *A Picture of Sarvodaya Social Order*, Akhil Bharat Sarva Seva Sangh Prakashan, Tanjore, 1956, p. 17
3. Jayaprakash Narayan, *Socialism to Sarvodaya*, Socialist Book Centre, Madras, 1956, pp. 30-31.
4. Jayaprakash Narayan, *Three Basic Problems of Free India*, Asia Publishing House, Bombay, 1974, p. 123.
5. Jayaprakash Narayan, *From Socialism to Sarvodaya, op. cit.*, pp. 11-12.
6. Jayaprakash Narayan, *Why Socialism, op. cit.*, p. 3.
7. General Secretary's Report of the Sixth Annual Conference of the Socialist Party, Nasik, 1948, p. 98.
8. Jayaprakash Narayan, *Socialism, Sarvodaya and Democracy, op. cit.*, p. 46
9. *Ibid.*, pp. 46-47.
10. Jayaprakash Narayan, *From Socialism to Sarvodaya, op. cit.*, p. 37.
11. Jayaprakash Narayan, *A Picture of Sarvodaya Social Order, op.cit.*, p. 28.
12. Report of the Sixth Annual Conference of the Socialist Party, Nasik, 1948, p. 96.
13. Jayaprakash Narayan, *Socialism, Sarvodaya and Democracy, op. cit.*, p. 146.
14. Jayaprakash Narayan, *Towards Total Revolution*, Vol. I, *op. cit.*, pp. 227-28.

4

JAYAPRAKASH NARAYAN ON DEMOCRACY

Jayaprakash Narayan remarked that in the existing circumstances, democracy is the best form of government. He criticizes Parliamentary democracy. To him democracy may be a government of the people and for the people but not by the people. People have a very limited choice to select from the candidates set up by the political parties. The system of election is very expensive and appalingly wasteful. It creates unnecessary passions and excitements and fails to elect good and able men.

Jayaprakash Narayan was of the opinion that the greatest fault of Parliamentary democracy is its inherent tendency toward centralisation of power. He was of the opinion that in the modern states, individuals have no control over the government and finds himself reduced to a position of helplessness. The important issues in such states are decided by the political parties, industrialists, bankers and labour unions. To him parties often put group interests above the national interest and are run by the caucuses that are beyond democratic control. Party rivalries give rise to demagogy which eliminates political ethics.

According to Jayaprakash Narayan, a government which is elected under universal suffrage represents only the minority of the total voters where there is multi-party system. He reaches the conclusion that parliamentary democracy is formal democracy. He presents his scheme of government based on the principles of decentralisation, individual freedom and populat participation. He visualises a pyramidal structure of Indian polity based on a communitarian democracy composed on village communities as its basis. In his communitarian democracy, there is no place for political parties. He says that there may be political parties but they are likely to be-local fraction. Their role will not be commanding. The is maximum decentralisation of power. People will actively participate in the administration and will be accorded a central place. There will be no centralised state.

Jayaprakash Narayan recommendes a separation of legislative and executive powers. During the Total Revolution phase, he advocated the formation of people's committees in the villages and the cities. He gives full sovereign rights to the individuals. He laid emphasis on economic decentralisation. He agrees that the new democracy cannot be built in a day or two. There will be transition period. He agrees that education of the individual is of seminal importance for the success of true democracy. He was of the opinion that during the period of election campaign, masses may be educated, and insist that education should be imparted by non-governmental agencies.

Jayaprakash Narayan wants to revive the ancient concept of *Dharma* so that India may again be organised on the basis of self-determining and mutually co-ordinating and integrating communities. He does not take the positive stand that the philosophical revolution is a pre-condition of the success of Indian democracy. His total revolution implies comprehensive transformation of society in which the democratic values will permeate the political, economic and social spheres of life. His communitarian democracy will be a stateless society.

Jayaprakash Narayan called the concept of western democracy as democratic oligarchy. He criticized the Parliamentary system of democracy and he visualised the communitarian democracy. According to him, the first defect of parliamentary democracy is that it has atomised the society. He said, "the state cannot be an arithmetic sum of individuals. The people, the nation, the community can ever be equated with the sum of individual voters."[1] Parliamentary democracy is based on a negation of the social nature of man and the true nature of human society. He said, "The democracy conceives of society as an inorganic mass of separate gains of individual voter and the whole process of democracy rests on the arithmetic of votes. The individual voter casts his vote as an atom of society, not as a living cell in organic relationship with other living cells. It is not the living together that is expressed and represented in the institutions and process of democracy, but an abstracted individual."[2]

Under Parliamentary system the representative government is a minority government. This is another defect of democracy. On the basis of experience. Jayaprakash Narayan said, "That present-day mass elections manipulated by powerful, centrally controlled parties, with the aid of high finance and diablically clever methods and super media of communication represent for less the electorate than the forces and interests behind the parties and propaganda machines."[3]

Demagoguery is the next defect. According to Jayaprakash Narayan, politicians indulge in half-truths. They make dishonest pleasing promises to catch the votes. He said, "It also tends to involve prejudice, passions and emotions, which deform them; and to indulge in electoral outbidding which does not hesitate to sacrifice the good of the country, and even the real and long-term interests of the electors to their own immediate and apparent interests."[4]

The next defect in Parliamentary democracy according to Jayaprakash Narayan, is its inherent tendency toward centralism. He said, "The sovereign people being dispersed over the length and breadth of the country like particles of sand over the desert and having no other organised political force than the national state itself to interpose between themselves and that state, the latter naturally becomes all powerful. The issue of power in such state is decided not by the fictitions people but by a balance between, political parties and such organised interests as industrialists and bankers and powerful labour unions."[5]

In the Parliamentary democracy, the central executive is dependent upon bureaucrats, who gradually become all powerful. This tendency leads to autocracy. Jayaprakash Narayan said, "The peoples are not prepared to shoulder the responsibility of citizenship themselves, the responsibility of community life. They are content to cast their votes, they are content with throwing their votes to whoever they wish and then be satisfied with that. They have performed their duties as a citizen and therefore, nothing remains for them to do, the rest is for the states to do."[6] So, he insisted on more and more decentralisation.

According to Jayaprakash Narayan, the voters have no control over the parties. He believed that ordinary voters could not express their opinion intelligently on all the complicated issues that are placed before the people at the time of elections. He said. "And when we came to our own country with the backward electorate that we have—most of them illiterate, most of them are such that they have not travelled beyond their districts—is it possible for such persons to express their opinion on international affairs? Is it possible for them to give an intelligent answer?"[7] He condemned the party system.

The next defect of Parliamentary democracy is the system of election. Jayaprakash Narayan said. "The fabulous expenses involved have the effect of mortgaging democracy to moneyed interests or large sectional organisations as trade unions." In our country, elections have become increasingly irrelevant from the view-points of the people of democracy. Regarding the role of individual in democracy in India, he said, "Democracy in our country gives only this such right to the people that they cast their votes when an election comes round. Beyond this you and I have no other role as citizens in this democratic process. But this right is also snatched away from us since the elections are increasingly neither fair nor free". To him, Parliamentary democracy is inadequate democracy. Parliamentary democracy may be a government for the people and of the people, but it is not a government by the people.

In Jayaprakash Narayan's communitarian democracy there would be full political and economic decentralisation. There would be no role of political parties. He said, "What I have in mind is what Gandhiji often used to emphasize, namely that as you proceed from the bottom level of government to the top, each higher level should have less and less functions and powers. To back to the image of the inverted pyramid, the broad upper levels of present day democracy must be drastically sawed off and large portions of the vast upper floors brought down to earth, so that the pyramid—narrow at the top and broad at the bottom. In such a system the people at each level would have the fullest opportunity to manage all those affairs that might pertain to that level. Such a system of democracy could give people a stake in democracy as the sensation of *Swaraj.*

Jayaprakash Narayan laid down the following conditions for Panchayat Raj—education of the people, non-interference of the political parties, real devolution of power, allocation of minimum resources at each level of local authority, exercise of real control over civil servants under its charge and keeping the day-to-day working of Panchayat Raj outside the purview of the State Government. He advocated *Swaraj* from below as the basis of his picture of Indian polity. He said, "In the true community there is communion, i.e., sharing participation, fellowship, there is identity of interest; a feeling of unity in the midst of diversity: a sense of freedom within the framework of accepted social responsibilities: differentiation of functions converging to the single goal of the good of the community and its members."[11] Agriculture, industry, capital, labour, skill, intelligence would be synthesised in the service of the community.

A number of primary communities would come together and corporate amongst themselves to build regional community. Jayaprakash Narayan said. "At the regional level their is an integration of institutions and activities of the primary . . . just as in its internal administration the primary community is authonomous, so in the spheres in which the primary communities have delegated their powers to the regional community, the latter is autonomous."[12] The regional communities would have to come together to form the district community. The district communities in their turn would federate together to form the provincial community, and the union of provincial communities would emerge into the national community.

Jayaprakash Narayan laid stress on popular participation. He said, "I have been emphasising here the element of people's participation as a true measure of democracy. Now, if there is any level of self-government at which the fullest participation of the people is practicable, it is at the village level. It is only there that direct democracy can adequately function."[13]

Jayaprakash Narayan proposed the political structure for Indian Polity which would rise storey by storey from the base. The highest political institutions of the local community would be the *Gram Sabha* Every adult villager would be considered its member. It would elect the *Panchayat* to run the village administration. The next stage of the political structure would be regional community. The *Gram Panchayats* would have to be integrated into *Panchayat Samiti.* Next to *Panchayat Samiti* would be the District Council. It would be formed by the integration of the *Panchayat Samitis.* Next to District Councils, there would be State Assembly which would be formed by the integration of District Councils of a state. Finally, the State Assemblies would come together and form *Lok Sabha.*[14]

Jayaprakash Narayan suggested to give maximum powers to the communities so that people might learn and acquire self-confidence. That is why he said that police, justice, taxation, social services, planning should all be decentralised to the maximum possible extent. He suggested a tentative procedure for electing the State Assemblies and *Lok Sabha* as follows.

> "Each *Gram Sabha* in every constituency should elect at a properly convened general meeting, two delegates to an electoral college in the following manner. At that meeting nominations should be called for, and all the names proposed and seconded should be listed, preferably on a prominently displayed board . . each name should be voted upon—votes being taken by show of hands and the votes received by each nominee entered against his name on the board. Thereafter, there should be repeated balloting in order to eliminate all except two of the nominees. This might be done by dropping, at each ballot. the name receiving the least votes at the previous ballot and the remaining names."[15]

The Electoral Council's task would be to set up candidates for election. Jayaprakash Narayan said, "First there should be nominations, and then votes taken on each name proposed and seconded. Persons receiving not less than a given minimum of votes, say 30 per cent, should be declared to be the candidates from the constituency for the Vidhan or Lok Sabha as the case might be."[16] The Electoral Councils should try their best to set up not more than one candidate for every seat. If this does not happen to be practicable in some cases the names selected should be declared to be the candidates.

Final elections should be held as follows. "The names of the candidates selected by the Electoral Council should be sent to all the Gram Sabhas of the constituency concerned. Each *Sabha* should convene a general meeting where votes should be taken for each candidate. Thereafter one or two alternatives should be followed—(a) The candidate receiving the largest number of votes should be declared to be the person whom the particular *Gram Sabha* wants to represent it in the highest *Sabha.* Of all such persons the one receiving the largest number of *Gram Sabha* votes is finally declared to be the Member of the *Vidhan* or *Lok Sabha* from that constituency; (b) Alternatively, the votes received by each candidate at the general meeting of each *Gram Sabha* should be recorded. Then the votes that each has received at the different *Gram Sabha* meetings all over the constituency should be totalled. The candidate receiving the largest number of such votes then becomes the Member from that constituency."[17]

Jayaprakash Narayan advocated the formation of People's Committees in each Assembly constituency polling booth. Each people's committee from each polling-booth should send one representative selected by general consensus to an Assembly constituency People's Committee. He also suggested to organise *Gram Sabhas* in the countryside and neighbourhood and work councils in the cities and towns. According to him, these *Sabhas* would meet regularly, discuss their common problems and evolve co-operative and collective forms of action to manage their affairs. In State Assembly elections, he suggested the formation of a *Gram Sabha* Delegates Council.

Jayaprakash Narayan considered education as the most powerful means for creating self-regulated enlightened classes and stateless society of his concept. He did not like the present system of education. He believed that the primary aim of education should be to impart knowledge and training. It should aim at preparing the youth to earn his livelihood independently. To him, the true function of education would be to build a bridge between that inner and outer knowledge of individual so as to achieve a synthesis of understanding. He said, "When that happens, education might come into its own and be able to perform its true function of making both man and his environment, so that the outward and inward activities of man might come to be corelated and oriented to a common goal."[18]

Jayaprakash Narayan was of the opinion that the education should be practical as well as theoretical. He laid stress or rural education. He expected the educators of the people to come from all possible quarters. He said, "This education can best be imparted by disinterested, non-partisan agencies, engaged in social service or tasks of rural development. Political parties might also make a great contribution in this respect, provided they addressed themselves to the task in a non-partisan spirit. Perhaps the best way for them would be to create a common agency through which to carry on this work. Government officers and agencies might also do useful work in this sphere. Schools libraries, co-operative societies have an important role to play here."[19] He suggested for the formation of a non-party and purely educative body of voters.

REFERENCES

1. Jayaprakash Narayan, *A Plea for Reconstruction of Indian Polity*, Akhil Bharat Sarva Seva Sangh Prakashan, Kashi, 1959, p. 63.
2. *Ibid.*, pp. 47-48
3. *Ibid.*, p. 66
4. *Ibid.*, p. 67
5. *Ibid.*, p. 68
6. Jayaprakash Narayan, "Towards a Fuller Democracy', *The Radical Humanist*, Vol. XXII, No. 24, June 15, 1958, p. 282.
7. *Ibid.*
8. Jayaprakash Narayan, *A Plea for Reconstruction of India Polity, op. cit.*, p. 71.
9. Jayaprakash Narayan, *Total Revolution*, Akhil Bharat Sarva Seva Sangh Prakashan, Varanasi, 1975, p. 45.
10. Jayaprakash Narayan, *Swaraj for the People, op. cit.*, pp. 5-6.
11. Jayaprakash Narayan, *A Plea for Reconstruction of Indian Polity, op. cit.*, p. 50.
12. *Ibid.*, p. 57.
13. Jayaprakash Narayan, *Swaraj for the People, op. cit.*, pp. 15-16.
14. *Ibid.*, p. 42
15. *Ibid.*, pp. 42-43.
16. *Ibid.*, pp. 43-44.
17. *Ibid.*, pp. 44-45.
18. Jayaprakash Narayan, 'India and World Peace', *The Radical Humanist*, Vol. XXIX, No. 49, December, 19, 1965, p. 511.
19. Jayaprakash Narayan, *Swaraj for the People, op. cit.*, pp. 11-12.

5

LEADERSHIP OF JAYAPRAKASH NARAYAN

The dominant feature of Jayaprakash Narayan's political life extending over fifty years was a search for a revolution for equality and freedom. This objective made him to move first from Gandhi to Marx and then back to Gandhi. Towards the end of his life, he again entered the party and power politics, founding a Janata Party and campaigning for its success in the elections. He has left behind the outlines of a valuable political philosophy which will be found very useful for all those who want to work for a new social order in India.

Jayaprakash Narayan started his political career in 1921, as a fighter for Indian freedom under the leadership of Gandhi. Alongwith some other students, he walked out of the Patna College in order to join the freedom struggle. He received the ideals of brotherhood and equality from Karl Marx. He sailed for the United States in 1922. He stayed there for seven years, working in restaurants, factories, fields and studying at the universities of Wisconsin, Iowa, California and Ohio. He came in close contact with some communist students and converted to Marxism while he was studying at the University of Wisconsin.

Jayaprakash Narayan did not know that Gandhi also was seriously concerned with the problem of poverty. He said, "Marxism provided another beacon of light for me: equality and brotherhood. Freedom was not enough. It must mean freedom for all—even the lowliest—and this freedom must include freedom from exploitation, from hunger, from poverty."[1] One of the things that he did after his return to India from the United States was to pay a visit to Gandhi. He went to Lahore for attending the Annual Congress Session in 1929.

Jawaharlal Nehru appointed Jayaprakash Narayan as head of the newly created Department of Labour Research at the office of the AICC at Allahabad. He became a whole-time worker of the Congress. He could not play any role in the first civil disobedience campaign in

1930-31. He became the Acting General Secretary of the Congress in 1932. He maintained contact with the Congress workers in different parts of the country.

Jayaprakash Narayan became convinced that the socialist movement in India could not be carried on under the CPI or the guidance of the Comintern. Yusuf Meherally said, "Jayaprakash Narayan came out of prison with an idea, a purpose and a vision. And out of that was born the Congress Socialist Party."[2] This was started in 1934 with Jayaprakash Narayan as its General Secretary. This new party had branches all over the country.

The Congress Socialist Party's policy was drafted by Jayaprakash Narayan. He said, "The Congress Socialist Party grew out of the experiences of the last two national struggles. It was formed at the end of the last civil disobedience movement by such congressmen as came to believe that a new orientation of the national movement had become necessary, (as also) a redefinition of its objectives and a revision of its methods. The initiative could be taken only by those who had a theoretical grasp of the forces of our present society . . . The immediate task is to develop the national movement into a real anti-imperialist movement aiming at freedom from the foreign power and the native system of exploitation. For this it is necessary to wean the anti-imperialist elements in the Congress away from its present bourgeois leadership, and to bring them under the leadership of revolutionary socialism."[3]

According to Jayaprakash Narayan, *Socialism* is a system of social reconstruction and not a code of personal conduct. It cannot be established by a group of idealists without power. A socialist party in power can establish socialism provided it had ample power of coercion or sufficient popular support to deal with the opposition of vested interests. He strongly refutes the contention that socialism cannot be established in India because her traditions are different from those of the countries of Europe and she is economically very backward. He opines that if there is a socialist party in power, it can build up socialism in any part of the world.

While advocating the introduction of cooperative and collective farming, Jayaprakash Narayan visualises the village. He pointed out that the Indian people would need fewer labour-saving devices in view of their large population and shortage of land. He emphasised, under socialism, cities would be planned and concentration of too many people at one place would be avoided by dispersing industries. The village would cease to be merely an unit of agricultural production, and become also a unit of industrial production.

Jayaprakash Narayan attached particular importance to unity between the CSP and the CPI. He was so fascinated by the dream of socialist unity in India. He refused to countenance any change in the policy of admitting communists into his party even after coming across evidence of their enemical designs. The experience of working with communists had a lasting impact on his mind. It created in him a deep aversion to the communists and their methods.

Jayaprakash Narayan's activities during the Second World War mark him out as one of the heroes of the Indian liberation struggle and also illustrate his remarkable dedication to the cause of the freedom, his great courage and his capacity for sacrifice. He toured the country calling for total non-cooperation. It was for one of these speeches, he was arrested in 1940 and sentenced to imprisonment for nine months. His arrest created a stir in India. Gandhi said, "He (Jayaprakash Narayan) is no ordinary worker. He is an authority on socialism. It may be said that what he does not know of Western socialism nobody else in India does. He is a fine fighter. He has forsaken all for the sake of the deliverance of his country. His industry is tireless. His capacity for suffering is not to be excelled."[4]

Jayaprakash Narayan was once again arrested immediately after the nine months imprisonment was over, and kept in the special camp jail at Deoli. He undertook a fast in support of certain demands of the prisoners at Deoli. The fast continued for no less than thirty-one days and was broken only when the demands were fulfilled. He kept track of the onward march of the Indian struggle for freedom from his cell in the Hazaribagh Central Prison. With five other friends, he managed to scale the prison walls on 8 November, 1942.

Jayaprakash Narayan established contact with other freedom fighters in various parts of the country. His most significant contributions were his two letters to freedom-fighters in 1943. In his first letter, he exhorted the freedom-fighters not to be demoralised. When he issued his second letter he realised that the controversy on the issue of violence, if not checked, might prove to be a great source of discord and disruption in the ranks of the underground fighters for freedom. He tried to end that controversy by emphasising that every fighter should be free to choose his own means in order to make his contribution to the struggle and there need be no controversy regarding it.

Jayaprakash Narayan tried to organise a guerrilla force which he named *Azad Dasta.* While engaged in training the officer cadre of this force he was arrested by Nepal's police and was rescued by the trainees. He was arrested on 19 September, 1943, in a running train between Delhi and Rawalpindi. He was kept in Lahore Fort and he had to undergo a long period of interrogation and torture, and had to spend several months in solitary confinement. He was transferred to Agra Central Jail in January 1945 and was released in April 1946.

When Jayaprakash Narayan was released the British Cabinet Mission was already in India, engaged in negotiations with the Indian leaders. While the Congress leaders were busy with negotiations, he was touring the country, from one end to the other, carrying his message of struggle to vast masses of people. He managed to find time during his tour to issue his third letter to freedom-fighters on 9 August, 1946. He reiterated his conviction that freedom could not be achieved through negotiations. The top leaders of the Congress did not pay heed to his warnings and continued with the negotiations with the British. They were able to secure independence, but at a heavy price. He realised that the country had achieved independence and the time had come to wore seriously for bringing about a social revolution.

Although Jayaprakash Narayan did not challenge the theory of *violence* as a midwife for revolution in its entirety, it became quite clear to him that in a society where it was possible for the people by democratic means to bring about social change it would be counter-revolutionary to resort to violence, and that socialism could not exist, nor be created, in the absence of the democratic freedoms. As a logical corollary he rejected the theory of the dictatorship of the proletariat.

The attraction for Gandhian as well as Western democratic values increased in Jayaprakash Narayan's mind with the passage of time. He was more impressed by Erich Fromm's the Fear of Freedom. He appeared to like Fromm's views so much because they conformed to his own thinking at that time. He observed, "The human aspect which I have in mind goes beyond the question of social relationships which indeed will be largely, if not wholly, dictated by the nature of economic organisation; it goes beyond that of education and art and culture. That aspect goes deeper than all these and is their basis, viz. the character and type of men . . . in the field of character-building of a nation as in the economic field. Indeed, it seems doubtful if economic and political gains can become permanent without a concurrent development of the human material."[5]

The commingle of Marxism, Gandhism and Western democratic values in Jayaprakash Narayan's mind comes out best in two articles which he wrote in 1946. In the first article entitled "My Picture of Socialism", he describes himself as a Marxist. The second article, entitled "The Transition to Socialism" was published in 1947. Here he sets forth his ideas on how to achieve the goals.

In the later years the Gandhian component in Jayaprakash Narayan's political philosophy went on increasing, till a stage arrived when he disavowed his faith in dialectical materialism and proclaimed his adherence to Gandhi's philosophy of Sarvodaya describing it as a higher form of socialism. His transition from Socialism to Sarvodaya cannot be described as an abandonment of socialism, but only as an effort at the enrichment of its content and the discovery of a new path to it.

The transition from the Democratic Socialism to Sarvodaya took place gradually, over a period of time. As Jayaprakash Narayan watched the pursuit of power dominating the political scene more and more he began to ask himself whether power was really that important as to deserve so much attention on the part of public workers. Power achieved through immoral means could not become the means for ushering in a new society of morally upright human beings.

In 1951, Jayaprakash Narayan asked the socialists to make a careful study of the Sarvodaya plan for economic development. He expressed the hope that the Gandhians and socialists would join hands to find a new social order on that basis. He was fascinated by three aspects of Gandhism—its stress on moral or ethical values, its great contribution to revolutionary technology in the form of civil disobedience and satyagraha and its insistence on political and economic decentralisation. He felt that it was the duty of every scientific socialist, as distinguished from the dogmatist, to understand Gandhism and assimilate as much of it as found desirable in order to establish socialism.[6]

The abandonment of Dialectical Materialism cleared the way for a fuller adoption of Gandhism. Jayaprakash Narayan not only rejects the system of one-party dictatorship, but also finds shortcomings in the system of parliamentary democracy. He advocates the decentralisation of political power. According to him, the demerits of the Soviet economic system are centralisation, bureaucracy, lack of industrial democracy, lack of workers participation in the management of industry.

Jayaprakash Narayan argues that since the aim is the establishment of a democratic society, the means adopted to bring such a society into existence should also be democratic, of course, where such means are available. By democratic methods, he does not mean parliamentary methods, but also includes in them mass movements and actions of a non-violent character. He emphasises that the relationship between one socialist country and another must be one of mutuality and economic aid. He suggested that Gandhism should be utilised in order to develop the ideology of Socialism in India. He said, "Socialism wishes to advance by setting class against class, Gandhism by cutting across classes. Socialism wishes to destroy classes by making one class victorious over the other—which seems to be somewhat illogical. . . Gandhism like Socialism, aims at a stateless society."[7]

When Jayaprakash Narayan moved from one village to another with the message of *Bhoodan,* he had an experience similar to Vinoba's and was able to secure donations. He thought that the revolution by non-violent mass action taking place before his eyes. His fascination for the movement became so strong that he decided to devote all his time and attention to it, to the exclusion of everything else. This involved his withdrawal from the field of party and power politics. The socialists followed his lead and decided to leave the Congress at Nasik in March 1948. He took care to warn his fellow socialists against putting too much emphasis on capturing State power. He said, "We must remember today, and never forget it in the coming years that it would be by constructive work rather than by the tactics of a parliamentary opposition, by positive service rather than by exploiting the mistakes and faults of others, that we would succeed in establishing a democratic socialist society."[8]

Jayaprakash Narayan continued his effort to synthesise Gandhism with *Socialism.* In 'New Dynamics of Social Change', he emphasised that the failure to achieve socialism had been caused mainly by the adoption of wrong means. He observed that all of us agree that socialism is a way of life and attitude of mind, a certain ethical behaviour. What is not so universally recognised is that such a way of life, attitude, behaviour cannot be imposed from above by dictates of the government or by merely nationalising industry and abolishing capitalism. Construc-tion of a socialist society is fundamentally construction of a new type of human being. A socialist society is one in which the individual is prepared voluntarily to subordinate his interest to the larger interest of society. Such a society cannot be created through the old dynamics of social change based on a conflict of interests. He said that what is needed is not a dynamics based on a conflict of interests, but one that is based on the values of society that we all wish to create. What is needed is not so much a movement for the capture of power, but a movement that required that those who participated in it should begin here and now to live the new way of life.[9]

In his booklet *From Socialism to Sarvodaya,* Jayaprakash Narayan traced the evolution of his thought from the beginning of his political career and mentioned the reasons which finally led him to end all his association with party and power politics. Though he describes his transition from socialism to Sarvodaya, he does not look upon them as contrasting ideologies. He emphasises that the goals of both are the same; only the path of *Sarvodaya* is more likely to take us to those goals. In this sense he regards Sarvodaya as a higher form of socialism, but really looks forward to the day when the two would merge.

In 1958, Jayaprakash Narayan went on a tour of Europe and West Asia, meeting a number of leaders and thinkers in those parts of the world and visiting institutions of various types. This tour further convinced him that a copy of European political institutions would not solve India's problems. On return, he issued a statement emphasising that no nation could be built up without the massive participation of the people and drew attention to the undeniable fact that the people of India had not, on the whole, shown any enthusiasm for the official programmes of development.

In his 'A plea for Reconstruction of Indian Polity', Jayaprakash Narayan rejects the Western model of democracy on the ground that it does not give full scope to the people to participate in the management of their affairs and is based on an atomised society, the State being made up of an inorganic sum of individuals. He was unhappy with the dominant role played by the political parties in the country's affairs. According to him, the party system is productive of many evils—party rivalries give birth to demogoguery, depress political ethics, put a premium on unscrupulousness and aptitude for manipulation and intrigue. Parties create dissensions where they should be minimised. Parties often put party interests over the national interests. Because centralisation of power prevents the citizen from participating in government, the parties, that is to say, small caucuses of politicians rule in the name of the people and create the illusion of democracy and self-government.

Jayaprakash Narayan pleads for the replacement of parliamentary democracy by a new kind of polity. This he calls communitarian or partyless democracy. The essential attributes of a true community are sharing, participation and fellowship. The political structure of the community must correspond to its social structure and rise storey by storey from the foundation, which will consist of self-governing, self-sufficient, agro-industrial, urbo-rural local communities. The highest political institution of the local community should be the village assembly Gram Sabha. The executive should be selected by general consensus of opinion in the Sabha. The Sabha and the Panchayat should be given responsibility to manage things that really matter. The next level of the political structure will be Panchayat Samiti. Similarly, the Panchayat Samities of a district will be integrated into the District Council, the District Councils integrated into the State Assembly, and the State Assemblies integrated into the National Parliament. There will be indirect election.

In his *Swaraj for the People,* Jayaprakash Narayan stresses the urgency of the task of enabling the people directly to participate in the management of their affairs as far as possible. The role of the political parties should be restricted as far as possible and the people enabled to select their own candidates for election through popularly constituted Electoral Councils. He reiterates his view that the old belief of socialists that nationalisation of the means of production, distribution and exchange would automatically usher in economic democracy is no longer valid. The only solution is economic decentralisation.

Jayaprakash Narayan emphasises that he has been pleading for a decentralised economy because it would bring immediate benefit to the masses by offering employment on a mass scale and producing wealth in a manner that would ensure its wide distribution and make wage goods immediately available to ordinary consumers. In 1961 he expressed satisfaction that as a result of two five year plans the national income had increased as much as forty per cent, but pointed out that there had been no corresponding improvement in the condition of the common people.

Jayaprakash Narayan made a significant contribution to peace-making in Nagaland by serving as a member of the Nagaland Peace Mission in 1964-65. In 1967 he made serious efforts to usher in a politics of consensus at the national level. He appealed to the youth of the country towards the end of 1973 to enter the national arena and play a decisive role in establishing the primacy of the people and securing their victory over the power of money, falsehood and brute force. The student protest movement in Gujarat against widespread corruption there in the beginning of 1974 seemed to confirm his prognosis that the students were prepared now to act on wider issues.

In spite of illness Jayaprakash Narayan plunged into a mass struggle in Bihar in 1974, at the age of 72, primarily because of his conviction that such a movement was necessary in order to save democracy as well as to progress towards the goal of ushering a new society in India. In course of that struggle he had sometimes to work from his sick-bed and even to face lathi blows, but he never relented. He was arrested in June 1975. He wrote a letter to Indira Gandhi. He observed, "please do not destroy the foundations that the Fathers of the Nation, including your noble father, had laid down. There is nothing but strife and suffering along the path that you have taken. You inherited a great tradition, noble values and a working democracy. Do not leave behind a miserable wreck of all that. It will take a long time to put all that together again. For it will be put together again I have no doubt. A people who fought British imperialism and humbled it cannot accept indefinitely the indignity and shame of totalitarianism. The spirit of man can never be vanquished, no matter how deeply suppressed."[10]

Jayaprakash Narayan continued to work with the same determination to continue the struggle for both democracy and total revolution. In 1976 he observed, "Total revolution in permanent revolution. It will always go on and keep on changing both our personal and social lives. This revolution knows no respite, no halt, certainly not a complete halt. Of course, according to the needs of the situation its form will change, its programme will change, its processes will change. At an opportune moment there may be an upsurge of new forces which will push forward the wheels of change. The soldiers of total revolution must keep constantly busy with their programmes of work and wait for such an opportune movement."[11] In 1977 he persuaded the leaders of the major non-Congress and non-Communist parties to band together in the name of the Janata Party. He did not give up the struggle for either democracy or total revolution after the Janata Government was formed.

Jayaprakash Narayan's vision was not confined to India only, but encompassed the whole world. He keenly looked forward to India devoting herself assiduously to the causes of freedom and peace all over the world. His second letter to freedom-fighters in 1943 bears eloquent testimony to his lofty vision of India's role in the world as a crusader for freedom and peace. According to him, the future lay with the common people of the world, and India must seek to rally them together for strengthening the forces of peace and freedom.

REFERENCES

1. Bimal Prasad, *A Revolutionary's Quest: Selected writings of Jayaprakash Narayan*, Delhi, 1980, p. 183.
2. Yusuf Meherally, *Toward Struggle*, Bombay, 1946, p. 7.
3. Brahmanand, Jayaprakash Narayan, *Towards Total Revolution*, Vol. II, Bombay, 1978, pp. 1-2.

4. *Harijan*, 16-3-1940
5. Bimal Prasad, *A Revolutionary Quest*, n-1, Delhi, 1980, pp. 115-18.
6. Bimal Prasad, *Socialism, Sarvodaya and Democracy*, Bombay, 1964, pp. 91-96.
7. *Ibid.*, pp. 119-22.
8. Bimal Prasad, *A Revolutionary Quest*, n-1, Delhi, 1980, p. 145.
9. *Ibid.*, pp. 173-80.
10. Jayaprakash Narayan, *Prison Diary*, Bombay, 1977, p. 108.
11. Bimal Prasad, *A Revolutionary Quest*, n-1, Delhi, 1980, pp. 369-70.

6

JAYAPRAKASH NARAYAN ON TOTAL REVOLUTION

In 1942, under the leadership of Gandhiji, the Congress started the *Quit India Movement.* In 1974, Jayaprakash Narayan was asking the Congress rulers to leave their thrones, for they too had depoiled the country. This had taken the shape of total revolution. The central thrust of his campaign was against corruption in political life, but in its wider dimension, its aim was to assure the functioning of democracy in its true sense. The goal of total revolution coincides with the ideal of India's struggle for freedom.

In December 1973, Jayaprakash Narayan wrote to each member of Parliament suggesting ways and means to protect the citizen's fundamental rights. He addressed to the power of frustrated youth and appealed to them to launch a Youth for Democracy movement. He felt as strongly as ever about social injustice. His disenchantment with *Bhoodan* had begun, and he felt that the *Gram Swarajya* approach was not the right one The struggle approach was the right one. He does not share Vinoba's view point that systematic change in the political order should be brought about without a struggle, even a peaceful struggle. His experience of *Gram Swarajya* work had convinced him that *Gram Swarajya* is a valuable political organisation in itself provided it works and is not only on paper. But the *Gram Swarajya* movement was not capable of bringing about a systematic political revolution. He found remedy in peaceful people's struggle for revolutionary changes which would be more acceptable in Gandhi's India than elsewhere, and would not appear in the eyes of the revolutionary artists as Chimera.

Jayaprakash Narayan realised that students could be the answer to his search for social catalyst. A protest against bad food in a college hostel in Gujarat had snow balled into statewide campaign against political corruption that had brought down the State government, and brought about the dissolution of State legislature. The movement was started by students in Bihar also. They had twelve demands, of which eight related to minor university reforms, and the other four reflected the sufferings of the entire population. A demonstration by the students on 18 March, 1974 was countered by indiscriminate police violence. On the next day, the students action committee sought Jayaprakash Narayans's help and guidance. He agreed to guide them on two conditions—one was that they should be peaceful; and secondly, non-partisan. He said, "I do not believe that you can change man with violence, the change is only superficial. The only way to achieve permanent social change is through non-violence."[1]

Jayaprakash Narayan advised the students that violence would not work for tactical as well as for moral reasons. He asked students to give up one year of their education so that they can dedicate themselves to his movement of total revolution. The judgement of Allahabad High Court, invalidating the election of Mrs. Indira Gandhi on the grounds of corrupt practices and disqualifying her for next six years from having any election office, gave strength to the movement for total revolution. He allowed the demand of *Indira Hatao* to become the part of his movement. Opposition leaders and Jayaprakash Narayan expected the Prime Minister to resign with a view to establishing a sound moral and political convention. But Mrs. Gandhi refused to oblige. The opposition leaders in consultation with him chalked out a programme of *Satyagraha* for demanding her resignation.

On Mrs. Gandhi's refusal to resign, Jayaprakash Narayan found that democracy has ceased to exist in India. *Satyagraha* had become important for restoration of democratic system. A revolutionary change of the political system was an integral part of his movement for total revolution. The Government by declaring a state of internal Emergency, arresting Jayaprakash Narayan and other opposition leaders, issuing a series of ordinances which suspended the fundamental rights of the people, imposing press censorship and adopting draconian measures that upset the balance of constitution.

A revolutionary change of the political system was an integral and inseparable part of the total revolution and, therefore, of the struggle. The operation of internal Emergency lends weights to Jayaprakash Narayan's contention that it is not safe to restrict the functioning of democracy to elections, legislation, planning and administrative execution. So, he pleads that there must be people's direct action which would almost certainly comprise civil disobedience, peaceful resistance, non-cooperation in short, *satyagraha* in its widest sense. One of the unstated implications of such *satyagraha* would be self change; that is to say, those wanting a change must also, change themselves before launching any kind of action.

Jayaprakash Narayan was moving from the immediate to the ultimate aim of total revolution. He succeeded in the immediate objective of his movement by bringing various opposition parties together. This led to the formation of Janata Party and its victory in the Parliamentary elections, held in March 1977. Despite the role of Janata Party at the centre and most of the States, it will be possible to bring about any revolutionary change without the pressure and thrust of a movement. In the present context, a total revolution in India should mean a revolution from the village upwards to the largest urban concentration.

Jayaprakash Narayan's total revolution aims at comprehensive change, i.e., revolution in every sphere of social life and organisation. Total revolution is a combination of seven revolutions—social, economic, political, cultural, ideological or intellectual, educational and spiritual. For him, the process of revolution is very rapid, very far reaching and radical too, and sometimes it leads to qualitative change in the object of change. However, he makes it clear, the revolution being peaceful, it was not to happen suddenly and swiftly as the basic systematic change would happen first and the individual and group adaptations, most psychological later. He said, "To bring about a systematic change in society a revolution in every sphere and aspect of society became even harder when it had to be brought about peacefully, without impairing the democratic structure of society."[2]

The word total, to Jayaprakash Narayan is more akin to comprehensive. It covers the totality of life in its multifarious aspects. A revolution to be truly successful should bring about a radical change in the power from the group to another is no revolution. A truly successful revolution is that which transfer power not to a group, but to the people at large. His total revolution transfers total power to the people at large. Political and economic revolutions cannot be complete without a continuous process of change in the social and cultural field, and also in the educational field, reforming man himself intellectually and culturally, as well as morally or spiritually. A mere change in the system is not enough. It must necessarily accompany with a change in the individual man. The whole truth is that the system as well as the individual must undergo the process of change simultaneously, presenting the integral nature of total revolution.

Total revolution give new dimension to communitarian democracy. Jayaprakash Narayan suggested in setting up student and people's action *Samities* in all parts of the country. These *Samities* will mobilise public opinion, endorse candidates for legislature and work for his success. He shows preference for minimum government and maximum independent community initiative. He provides infrastructure of total revolution through these *Samities.* The politics of total revolution is the Politics of *Lokniti* and not *Rajniti* and this new politics will not be imposed from the top but will be built from below. His emphasis on the non-partisan character of his movement raises the question of partyless democracy which is the ultimate aim of total revolution.

Democracy cannot be practised through the intermediary of party politics. Jayaprakash Narayan laid emphasis on participation. In the immediate context of the movement for total revolution, he does not insist on partyless democracy. He advised the students and other participants to work unitedly and give the objectives of the movement priority over the programme of their parties. He insisted on the cooperation and participation of all sections of society. He believed that it is possible to develop a partyless democracy.

The concept of total revolution paves the way for the evolution of communitarian democracy in which the party system may become unnecessary. Jayaprakash Narayan depends upon the *satyagraha* to ensure the success of the movement for total revolution. According to Shri Dada Dharmadhikari, Jayaprakash Narayan's concept is hundred per cent relevant to *satyagraha* and his movement for total revolution was closer to Gandhi's *satyagraha* than any other movement of non-violent resistance in recent history. The total revolution is to be brought about not by rowdyism but by orderly *satyagraha,* self-sacrifice.

Experience had convinced Jayaprakash Narayan that Indian Constitution as it had actually evolved was incapable of functioning as an instrument of social change. He had experienced the futility of violence in his career. He was fully conversant with its theory and practice, and had given up that path after mature consideration. Vasant Nargolkar said, "under the existing circumstances, violence will lead to anarchy. Unless the widespread discontent in the country is channelised into a peaceful struggle, it will express itself in sporadic violence, and this will make it easy for whosoever is there at the head of the government to clamp down a dictatorship."[3] Gandhian *satyagraha* is the thrust of Jayaprakash Narayan's movement for total revolution.

REFERENCES

1. Jayaprakash Narayan on his movement in Bihar, *The Radical Humanist,* Vol. 38, No. 5, 1975, p. 10
2. Ajit Bhattacharjea, *Jayaprakash Narayan: A Political Biography,* Vikas Publishing House, New Delhi, 1978, p. 211.
3. Vasant Nargolkar, *J.P. Vindicated,* S. Chand & Company, New Delhi, 1977, p. 37.

7

JAYAPRAKASH NARAYAN ON PEACE

Jayaprakash Narayan advocated world peace and good friendly relations among the countries. He criticized communism, imperialism, fascism and other expansionist systems. He laid stress on principles of self-determination, non-involvement and non-interference. He condemned war as a means to settle international disputes. He reacted to the issues involving violence and suppression. He always condemned the big powers for intervening in the affairs of the small countries. He criticized the competitive race for armament. He was a loyal follower of Gandhi and his ideal of nationalism though he never supported the aggressive brand of nationalism and formulated his views on world peace within the framework of an international community comprising of nation-states. He opposed assisting Britain in the European War. To him, it was an imperialist war and not a people's war.

Jayaprakash Narayan advocated for peace, disarmament, amicable settling of the disputes and friendly relations between the countries. He said, "The free Indian nation shall work for peace between nations and total rejection of armaments and for the method of peaceful settlement of national disputes through some international authority freely established. It will endeavour particularly to live on the friendliest terms with its neighbours whether they be great powers or small nations, and shall covet no foreign territory".[1] In 1960, he pleaded for creating a non-violent social order internally and raising of a *Shanti-Sena* for non-violent defence through martyrdom, externally.

Jayaprakash Narayan encouraged the growth of a Non-aligned world in 1950's. In 1960's, he developed the concept of a Fourth World. He urged immediate and effective steps towards general disarmament and self-determination for small nations. In 1975, he warned the non-aligned and socialist countries. He condemned the imperialism of both the capitalist and the communist countries. He said, "There are feudalism, capitalism, imperialism, *totalitarianism.*

There are caste and colour, rich and poor, learned and illiterate. All these are forms of expression of violence. As long as they remain, there will be violence in the world and there will be wars."[2]

Jayaprakash Narayan believed in international *disarmament*, the destruction of all atomic, chemical and biological weapons, and unilateral disarmament for India. In 1950, he condemned the American aggression in Korea. To him, the two great powers, U.S.S.R. and the U.S. stood on the two sides, and the Koreans were merely pawns in the game. He was of the opinion that every country should be independent, and no country should attack or interfere in the matters of another country. In 1961, he criticized the Government of India for marching troops into Goa. He tried to foster an agreement of friendly relations and brotherhood between the people of India and Pakistan. He stressed the need for *conciliation* with Pakistan. In 1965, he condemned Pakistani aggression on Kashmir. He stressed the need of a solution within the Indian Union and maximum autonomy for Kashmir.

Jayaprakash Narayan advocated non-violent means to face Chinese aggression. He said, "Non-violence is the only answer to the situation of the world is facing today. Our means of peaceful settlement like negotiations across the table, good offices, adjudication, arbitration, friendship march and similar methods may succeed, or may fail—but there is no failure for a people who have accepted non-violence and have prepared themselves to resist whatever evil that might come, with non-violence".[3] He suggested the Indian Government to disarm unilaterally, to demobilise the Indian army and to take weapons of non-violence in place of violent arms. He emphasised non-violent method to meet the Chinese aggression.

According to Jayaprakash Narayan, India would endanger the cause of peace if she joined the power blocs. To solve the boundary dispute between India and China, he sought to find some impartial judges or arbitrators in whom both of us have trust and refer this boundary issue to them. He organised a Peace March from Delhi to Peking. In 1963, he said, "Though India is preparing for military defence, we should realise that armaments offer no real defence; rather they only lead to a ruinous race in armaments and to a succession of wars each more destructive than the last. What kind of security is there in that."[4]

Jayaprakash Narayan undertook a tour round the principal capitals of the world to awaken the international conscience against the killing of the people in Bangladesh. He advocated recognition of Bangladesh immediately. On behalf of the Sarva Seva Sangh and the Gandhi

Peace Foundation, he went on a mission of peace, from 16 May to 27 June 1971, to Cairo, Rome, Moscow, Belgrade, Stockholm, Paris, Bonn, Washington, London, New York, Vancouver, Ottawa, Tokyo, Kuala Lumpur, Jakarta and Singapore. He criticized the United Nations Organisation for its failure in restraining the great powers. He stressed the need to discover a surer way for safeguarding human liberty and the security and independence of nations.

REFERENCES

1. Jayaprakash Narayan, *Socialism, Sarvodaya and Democracy*, Asia Publishing House, Bombay, 1946, p. 37.
2. Allan and Wendy Scarfe, *J.P.: His Biography*, Orient Longman, New Delhi, 1975, p. 404.
3. Jayaprakash Narayan, *Sarvodaya Answer to Chinese Aggression*, Sarvodaya Prachuralaya, Tanjore, 1963, p. 18.
4. *The Search Light*, 25 May, 1963.

8

JAYAPRAKASH NARAYAN AND BHOODAN MOVEMENT

In the early fifties, Jayaprakash Narayan was subjected to two contrary influences, one, his link with the socialist party was becoming weaker as a result of petty squabbles among the leadership, the second was the magnetism of Vinoba's *Bhoodan* movement. Step by step, he severed his ties with the party and threw himself into *Bhoodan,* not merely as a method of peaceful land redistribution but also to lay the foundations of a partyless form of democracy in which decisions were taken by consensus on the model of the village panchayat. He was searching for an effective non-violent instrument for social change, but found it neither in Marxism nor in Parliamentary democracy.

In the first Asian Socialist Conference in Rangoon, Jayaprakash Narayan said, "I do not find today Gandhiji's dynamism and incessant quest towards his ultimate values except in Vinoba, who produced a remarkable Gandhian method for the solution of the country's biggest problem, the land problem." The inevitable occurred in 1954. At a *Sarvodaya* Conference at Bodh Gaya, where Lord Buddha found enlightenment, he announced that he had become Jeevandani.

Indeed, Jayaprakash Narayan started speaking on *Bhoodan, Gramdan* and *Gram Swarajya* with enthusiasm of a new convert and with zeal of a missionary: Bhoodan is an agrarian movement, which at best, is preparing the ground for *legislation*. To those who have looked deep, it is far more significant movement. It is the beginning of an all-round social and human revolution because it aims at changing man along with society. It is an application on a general scale, of Gandhiji's non-violent technique of revolution. Bhoodan is a great mass movement of conversion and creation of a new climate of thought and values of life. It brings about a living and immediate revolution in the minds of men and their mutual relationships. It attacks and corrects here and now the system of exploitation and inequality. It teaches men to share what they have, with their fellowmen. In the beautiful revolution of Gramdan, ownership was not abolished by force of any kind, but freely surrendered to the community. The outward social change was accompanied with inward human change. It is an example of what Gandhiji meant by double revolution. In place of social tensions, conflicts and tyrannies there were freedom and mutual goodwill and accord, making it possible for an unprecedented output of free collective initiative and endeavour. As I see it, it is a two-pronged method, one prong of it is mass campaign of what Gandhiji termed conversion. A widespread campaign is launched to persuade men, irrespective of class, creed and other differences, to give up those ideas, ways and values of life that have been found to be wrong and harmful and to accept in their place certain others. Thus, a revolution in ideas and values is set in motion. At the same time, the new values and ideas are so chosen that they have a direct bearing on some major social problems and their acceptance and practice are expected to lead to a solution of that problem and incidentally to radical change in society. The other prong of the method is to devise a programme of self-help and self-government through which men living in small communities may learn to manage their own affairs and forms of social life.

Jayaprakash Narayan interpreted Gandhian ideas and tried to emphasize the relevance of trusteeship, non-violence, satyagraha and of Gandhiji's rural industries programme. His main purpose was to evolve a policy of *Sarvodaya* approach and the efficiency of the various ways available for the reconstruction of Indian polity. Inspite of differences in personality traits of Gandhiji and Jayaprakash Narayan (1) the latter was convinced of Gandhiji's open mindedness and catholicity; (2) Spirit of exploration to search for an alternative to violent change; (3) Importance of people oriented struggle as a means of awakening people's power; (4) The concept of dual strategy of change and of a parallel polity. It is interesting to note that Jayaprakash Narayan learnt from Gandhiji, the need for a creative equilibrium between constructive and combative activities. According to him, continuing constructive activity builds up the strength to resist evil and injustice and opens up unlimited reservoirs of strength and sharpens social awareness and help to give decisive orientation. Establishment of a number of voluntary agencies and the Bihar movement are examples of Jayaprakash Narayan's counterpart of Gandhiji's *satyagraha* and constructive work.

According to Jayaprakash Narayan, the role of voluntary social welfare organisations is not merely to build establishment-oriented institutions, but also to catalyse its clientele to bring in fundamental social change. Mass contacts in society and to win people's confidence, to create moral sanctions in society, to involve people in the task of reconstruction and train them for non-violent action are the functions of voluntary agencies, as conceived by him. Above all, his concepts of *Jana-sakti* and *Janata sarkar,* which he evolved in 1974 and in 1975 were his major contributions in the field of innovational efforts, during the Bihar movement.

Jayaprakash Narayan not only classified and amplified but also commented on the seminal ideas of Gandhiji and he restated his opinions on class struggle and made a plea for incorporating the same within the Gandhian strategy for change. Some important contributions of Jayaprakash Narayan's Total Revolution are (1) Lok Samitis; (2) Sampoorna Kranti; (3) Class Struggles involving organisations of the rural poor for non-violent struggles; (4) *Lok Samitis* to struggle for the weaker sections. By 1959, he realised the concept of sharing remained confined to the agrarian sphere or land reforms field. He was thinking how in the field of industry, commerce and professions, the social workers could go forward from sharing of incomes to new kinds of organisations, where there is human fellowship, since human relationships binds and run the organisations and also govern their life and working.

Jayaprakash Narayan's main objectives for total revolution were two fold and they are: (1) How to make the present democratic system get rid of its inadequacies and to make it function more effectively in the interests of freedom, equality and fraternity. (2) How to change the entire system in India in a fundamental sense and to bring about total revolution in order to ensure freedom, equality and fraternity. Although he was disillusioned with the working of the democratic system in India and elsewhere, he remained at heart a liberal, notwithstanding his Marxism and he used liberally Gandhiji's ideas and prescriptions to temper his liberalism, as is evident in his *Reconstruction of Indian Polity.*

Bhoodan is really a development of Gandhian concept of *satyagraha* or revolutionary application of truth and non-violence to the present day problems of social and economic injustice and social transformation. In its wider and ideological sense, Bhoodan includes all other similar activities such as *Sampatidan, Shramdan* and *Buddhidan.* The use of the word *Dan* is perhaps unfortunate, for the reason that it creates the misunderstanding that Vinoba was merely asking for charity. He, of course, was using the word in its classical sense, in the sense of equal distribution. Therefore, it is necessary first of all to understand that Bhoodan is not a charity movement, but behind it is Gandhiji's theory of trusteeship.

Bhoodan movement does not aim at capturing the state in order to use it for its ends. It insists that if our ultimate aim is to do without the state, we must here and now create those conditions in which the people will rely more and more on themselves and less and less on the state. A movement that aims so utterly to revolutionise man and society cannot be but political. But, it is not politics of parties, elections, parliaments and governments, but policies of the people not *raj-niti* but *lok-niti,* says Vinoba.

The ultimate goal of the Bhoodan movement is not mere giving out patches of land to the landless but bringing about a real change of heart among the 'haves' to share their wealth with the 'have-nots'. The most vital problem facing the human race at the moment is the moral problem. It is not, so much a political or economic problem as the problem of standards of values that human beings throughout the world face. The Bhoodan movement is an answer or rather an attempt to solve the problem facing them now. A real and lasting change in the social order can be brought about only by a real change of heart and we should take a lesson in that respect from the French and Russian revolutions.

Misery in the world is not due to shortage of provisions and amenities, which science can multiply to any extent but due to the narrowness and possessiveness of man. There is misery not because there is no production but man is self-centred and does not think of others. This sort of life results in preparation for war. The problems seeingly political are in fact moral. The possessive instinct has to be weeded out by all. Rich and poor alike are victims of the craving for acquiring wealth, both adore the same values. That is why Vinoba insisted on receiving Bhoodan even from small land-holder and *Sampatidan* from everybody, rich and poor.

9

JAYAPRAKASH NARAYAN AND SARVODAYA

Jayaprakash Narayan's interest in Bhoodan movement grew in 1951 when he met Vinoba and came closer to the Sarvodaya philosophy. In 1957, he left active politics and devoted his full time in the *Bhoodan* Movement. The main reason for this decision was frustration and disillusionment due to the growing disintegration and conflict within the Socialist movement. This marked his transformation from socialism to *Sarvodaya.* He contributed in the development of the concepts of Gramdan and Jeevandan.

Jayaprakash Narayan had long been searching for an effective non-violent instrument for social change, but found it neither in Marxism nor in Parliamentary Democracy. So he took readily to the thesis that land reforms and village democracy could be set up by persuasion and conciliation that appeared to be the only way out. He went to the extent of linking Socialism with Sarvodaya for the achievement of a true socialist order. He said, "However, some years back it became clear to me that socialism as we understand it today cannot take mankind to the sublime goals of freedom, equality, brotherhood and peace. Socialism, no doubt, give promise to bring mankind closer to those goals than any other competing social philosophy. But I am persuaded that unless socialism is transformed into Sarvodaya these goals would remain beyond its reach; and just as we had to taste the ashes of independence, so future generations may have to taste the ashes of socialism".[1]

Jayaprakash Narayan did not lose his faith in socialism. This can be found in his views on the decentralisation of economic power. He said, "And that is possible only when there is decnetralisation in the economic field. When the system of production is organised on the basis of village industries and the large-scale industries, that will have to be essentially retained, will be socially owned and managed by workers."[2] He pleaded for simple living. He said. "We should realise that Gandhiji's philosophy of production was inseparable from his philosophy of consumption. Some people make the mistake of thinking that we can adopt the Gandhian mode of production and economic organisation without insisting on the Gandhian mode of consumption and living. But this cannot be done. Once the slogan of a high standard of living and equality are given without qualification, it becomes nearly impossible to restrain mass demand for the high level of consumption and the extravagant style of living, which only a minority enjoys in the beginning."[3]

Jayaprakash Narayan wanted the village panchayat to be autonomous and charged with the task of looking after the welfare of the people. He said, "If there is real Gram Raj established in a village, it should be the responsibility of that Gram Raj to see that everyone in that village is well-fed, well-clothed and fully employed. Now the only way for this to be done is by abolishing individual ownership of land and establishing community ownership by the development of home and village industries. Hunger can be banished from the village only when it is accepted that every member of the village has a right to the village land and to the produce of these lands."[4] He said that if we want to find a society of the 'Free and equal', then we have got to create units of self-sufficient villages and learn to take unanimous decisions. That means we have to create reservoirs of non-violent strength of the people.

Jayaprakash Narayan was of the opinion that the conservation of economic resources should not be viewed from the point of the present needs but also the needs of the future generations, who have the equal rights over them. He said, "Just as the father is concerned with not only providing for the present needs of his wife and children but is also concerned with providing for their future needs, in like manner must the community think not only of the present generation but also of the future generations. It must be careful of the non-renewable resources of nature: oil, coal, metal—these are some of the non-renewable resources. If the economy exploits these indiscriminately, there will be none of these left for use by the future generations. An economy that wants to provide for the future must, therefore, strive to live in harmony with nature. It must restrict consumption as far as possible to renewable resources and use as little as possible the resources it cannot give back to nature".[5]

Jayaprakash Narayan pleaded for the maintenance of the conditions that are necessary for the realisation of equality of opportunities He believed in the primacy of economic problems and their equitable solution. He stressed the elimination of the restraints, both mechanical and social, that hamper the productivity in Indian agriculture. He said, "An economy, based on mass production with a desire to have more and more, creates a baffling 'vastness' in society, in which the individual gets lost. An economy of limited works is thus desirable because it helps the all-round and balanced development of personality, and saves us from the evils of corruption and perdition".[6]

REFERENCES

1. Jayaprakash Narayan, *From Socialism to Sarvodaya,* Akhil Bharat Sarva Seva Sangh Prakashan, Kashi, 1959, p. 26.
2. Jayaprakash Narayan, *A Picture of Sarvodaya Social Order,* Sarvodaya Prachuralaya, Tanjore, 1957.
3. Jayaprakash Narayan, *Towards a New Society,* Sarvodaya Prachuralaya, Tanjore, 1957, p. 52.
4. Jayaprakash Narayan, *A Picture of Sarvodaya Social Order, op. cit.,* p. 76
5. Jayaprakash Narayan, *A Plea for the Reconstruction of the Indian Polity,* Akhil Bharat Sarva Seva Sangh Prakashan, Kashi, 1959, pp. 74-75.
6. *Ibid.,* pp. 5-6.

APPENDIX

TOTAL REVOLUTION (JAYAPRAKASH NARAYAN)

I

Since independence, there has been no real change in the social, economic and political structure of our society. *Zamindari* is abolished, land reform laws have been passed, untouchability has been legally prohibited, and so on. But, the village in most parts of India is still in the grip of the higher castes and the bigger and the medium landowners. The small and the marginal landowners and the landless, the backward classes and the Harijans—these form the majority in most villages in most States, perhaps in nine-tenths of India. Yet their position continues to be miserable. *Harijans* are still burnt alive. The *Adivasis* are still the most backward section, barring the Harijans. And the money-lenders mercilessly cheat and exploit the Adivasis, who in Bihar call the plainsmen *dikku.*

Some industries, banks, life insurance have been nationalised. Railways were nationalised long ago. New large public-sector industries have been established. But all this adds up to State capitalism and inefficiency, waste and corruption State capitalism means more power to the State, mainly the State bureaucracy or what Galbraith aptly calls the public bureaucracy'. There is no element or trait of socialism in all this. The working class and the public or, let us say, the people have no place in all this except as workers or consumers. There is no economic democracy, which is so much talked about, nor even industrial democracy. This does not mean that I am opposed to socialism. It is only because I am so deeply concerned about socialism that I am pointing all this out. It is a pity that our socialists very largely equate socialism with nationalisation.

The educational system in spite of several committees and commissions remains basically what it was during British rule: class education designed as an escalator to reach the top. There is so much to say about this, but this is not the place. Here I am trying only to show that the structure of society has remained unchanged through the years since independence.

The customs, manners, beliefs, superstitions, all these remain much the same for the masses. Even among the classes the change is superficial in most parts.

Since independence there has been a steady decline in political, public and business morality.

If we take social and economic development, the pciture is frightful. Population growth goes racing forward. Poverty is also growing: more than 40 per cent of the people are below the poverty line. The barest necessities such as drinking water, man-worthy and not cattle-worthy housing, medical care, apart from food and clothing, are not available. Schools are few and the teaching is bad. The papers say today that Bihar is the richest State in the country in minerals. Bihar also has good land and perennial rivers. Why then is Bihar, the poorest State in India? Well, one could go on adding to the list.

The question is, can the picture be fundamentally altered through the ordinary democratic process? Even if the Opposition wins, will the picture change? I fear, no, laws will be passed and applied, moneys will be spent—even if all this is done, possibly without corruption creeping in, will the structure, the system, the 'order' of our society change? I think, no why?

Before, I answer let me elucidate what I mean by a few examples. Take the marriage customs, particularly the *tilak* and *dahez* system, prevalent in Bihar, Bengal, Uttar Pradesh and some other States. This evil has been sought to be corrected by law, but the law has been a dead letter. Meanwhile the disease is growing fast, ruining many families and ruining the lives of many girls. Castes that had till the other day been free of this evil are rapidly falling a prey to it, because what is, social evil appears to them to be a status symbol. There is no remedy but a vigorous social movement, a peaceful struggle against the evil. Likewise, the implementation of land reforms, homestead tenancy legislation, removal of corruption in the administration, etc. All this requires a mass awakening and a mass struggle. The youth, including the students must naturally be in the vanguard.

II

The question is even larger. It is how to bring about a systematic change in society; i.e., how to bring about what I have called a total revolution: revolution in every sphere and aspect of society. The question becomes harder to answer when it is added that the total revolution has to be peacefully brought about without impairing the democratic structure of society and affecting the democratic way of life of the people. Put in this way, even the most legalistic and constitutionalist democrat would agree that all this could never be accomplished if the functioning of democracy were restricted to elections, legislation, planning and administrative execution. There must also be people's direct action. This action would almost certainly comprise, among other forms, civil disobedience, peaceful resistance, non-cooperation—in short, *satyagraha* in its widest sense. One of the unstated implications of such *satyagraha* would be self-change: that is to say, those wanting a change must also change themselves before launching any kind of action.

I recall Chandra Shekhar several times asking me what the Bihar movement, or any other such movement, would achieve if it were only to replace the Congress government by the Opposition. Will that government be any better? It was a valid question, which the Opposition parties should ponder. There performance in 1967 was certainly a great disappointment.

My answer to Chandra Shekhar used to be that the movement's aim was not only to change the government in Bihar, but much more which I had 'capsuled' in the term 'revolution'. The movement would go on, which in itself would be a poweful guarantee of the Opposition government always being on its toes, and that it would go on faster and smoother because the new government would give its full cooperation. In fact, a point to stress here is—and this I have done so often in the course of the Bihar movement—that had the Bihar government at the outset decided to cooperate with the students in examining and attempting seriously to solve the problems they had highlighted in their twelve demands, there would have been no question of the Bihar student's movement wanting to remove the Bihar Government. As is well known by now, the demand for the removal of the ministry and the Assembly came much later as a result of the violence, repression and lies let loose by the then Bihar Government.

The upshot of what I have been saying is that the people's movement of the type I am visualising here can proceed either in cooperation or in confrontation with the government concerned. I enunciated this principle clearly for the first time in my speech at the civic reception at Poona (on 23 January 1975). But this was not a thought that had suddenly dawned upon me at the reception. It had always been present in my mind and I am sure I had spoken several times before about it. But because of the fact that the Poona Municipal Corporation, though in the hands of the Opposition with a socialist Mayor, had ruling Congress members too within its fold and they too had voted for my reception, I thought it necessary to enunciate that principle as clearly as possible. For the Poona press it was something new and they highlighted it and it was very well reported in the national press. That is why it was thought at that time that I had made a new departure. Indeed, it appeared like that to some Opposition leaders in Bihar too. But the very procedure laid down for the starting of a movement implicitly accepted this position. First, a number of demands that are most important for the people are drawn up and they are presented to the Chief Minister. If upon that the Chief Minister were to say, "Well, all right let us sit together and work this out; I am prepared to cooperate with you in solving these problems and removing these evils"—corruption in the ministry, for instance—the struggle takes the course of cooperation. So far, not a single Congress Government has chosen to follow this course. More often, there is no reply at all or if there is, it is evasive and beside the point.

III

Thus, my concept of struggle need not inevitably include a struggle against the government of the State It is up to the government concerned to decide what policy it will follow: that of cooperation or of confrontation. The question is, why have the Congress government, wherever faced with a people's charter of demands, never found it possible to adopt the path of cooperation? The answer, as I indicated in my letters to the Prime Minister lies in the corruption among Congress ministers. Mrs. Gandhi's own conduct in collecting crores of rupees from rich businessmen for party and election management is a piece of political corruption that has completely destroyed the moral susceptibilities of most powerseeking Congressmen. Party and election funds were collected in Jawaharlal's time also, in Shri Babu's time also (to speak only of Bihar, but it was done everywhere), but the scale of operations was comparatively small and most of the money was accounted for. In any case, it never happened that only Jawaharlal knew how much was collected; others also like Sardar Patel or S.K. Patil knew it. Nor were business bargains struck in the process so shamelessly corrupt as those of which one has heard in Mrs. Gandhi's time.

Be that as it may, corruption being the focal point of the recent student's and people's movements, and the Congress ministries in the states or at the centre not being prepared to face the issue, they could not adopt the consistently hostile attitude they have adopted to the movement. There was also perhaps a stronger reason, though it was not visible. When the Congress found that the movement was not going to be satisfied with superficial remedies but that it was also aiming to bring about basic fundamental changes in society, including basic political changes in short, a total revolution—it was too much for it to stomach opposition from the Government was natural, through raising a cloud of dust about 'danger to democracy'; danger of 'internal disturbance', etc.

The question is, will the opposition parties behave differently? That is yet to be seen. But having once joined the movement, no doubt to exploit it for party and election purposes (which is in the very nature of political parties), they find themselves not only committed to the final goal of total revolution but also being radicalised in the process of the struggle. Even about exploiting the movement for party ends, I cannot deny that they have tried to do so in Bihar—the better organised and disciplined the party, the more guilty it has been. But in the total picture, it will not be wrong to say that the interests of the struggle have been generally placed above the interests of the party. The only exceptions are places where only one party holds sway and the non-party forces among the students, citizens and the local Sarvodaya workers are weak; the party in question has in that case identified its party interests with the interests of the struggle. It was precisely with a view to strengthening the non-party forces that I had been busy organising a new volunteer force of non-party youths and students called Chhatra Yuva Sangharsha Vahini. A big rally of these youths was to be held and addressed by me at Patna on the day of my arrest, 26 June, 1975.

There is one difficulty about this concept of peaceful social or total revolution. Can the necessary psychological climate of struggle be created at will? If not, the struggle of this concept is as unlikely to get off the ground as Vinobaji's movement for *gram swarajaya.* True, the pre-conditions for a social struggle (using the term social in its widest sense) are always present in poverty, unemployment, miseducation, etc. But still there is need for a spark to kindle the fires of struggle, to set alight the dry tinder-box of Indian society.

There is another minor difficulty too. That is about the non-Congress and non-C.P.I. Opposition parties. Unless a struggle involves struggle against the Congress Government they will not feel attracted towards it, because in the case it hardly promises any dividends. Indeed, they might fear that if the struggle is against the vested interests (as it must be to have any meaning), their participation in it might adversely affect their electoral chances. This may not be true of some of the left parties, however.

Is there an answer to these difficulties? Yes, if we start writing on a clean slate. The future struggle must be related to the past struggle and the thread picked up where it had been dropped when the arrests were made and the Emergency was clamped down. The longer the fighters are kept in prison, the better would it be for resumption of the struggle. It is difficult at this stage to guess when, if at all, the general elections to the Lok Sabha and the Vidhan Sabhas will be held. 'If at all' in the preceding sentence is perhaps a wrong presumption, in her statements and interviews in the last two months Mrs. Gandhi has repeatedly committed herself to holding elections. When is the question. From her point of view the right time will be when the opposition is sufficiently demoralised and the people won over by her 20-point programme and sugared words and announcements of dazzling policies—which like fireworks will dazzle for a moment, then leave everything behind just as it was before. Whenever that moment comes for Mrs. Gandhi, the election dates will be announced and the detenus released. With all the Opposition leaders and other detenus remaining in jail, the election would be an utter farce. It would be difficult for Mrs. Gandhi to persuade public opinion in India and abroad particularly in the west, that elections under such conditions could ever be an exercise in democracy. Not even the British dared to do that in India.

Now, whatever happens in other States, the congress has no chance in Bihar in a free and fair election. Then, with a pro-struggle government established, the struggle would be resumed again. (By the way, this could be done in Gujarat today, but there seems to be no one there to relate the Navanirman movement to the present most favourable political situation in that State.) However, it may be Bihar's opportunity and good fortune to show how a society could be changed with the active cooperation between the people and the government.

Here I must comment on the usual talk of 'cooperation of the people', 'participation of the people', etc. Mrs. Gandhi is also indulging a great deal in such talk and Mr. (D.K.) Borooah—yes, the inevitable Mr. Borooah is busy setting up committees of the people to do this. In the heyday of Community Development this was common claptrap. But we who were working at the ground level then—in the villages—discovered what all that meant. It did not mean any initiative on the part of the people; it only meant that better off people in the village drained off everything or almost everything that the development pipeline was bringing to the people.

The case I am visualising for Bihar would be different. The struggle committees, the Janata Sarkars would pick up the thread where it was broken and beginning with the items of the movement's programme as it stood at that moment, they would forge ahead towards the goal of total revolution, the State government helping where its help was needed and taking help where it needed help itself. It is an exciting picture and I do pray to God to be spared to play such part as I may in this historic process.

What about other States? Well, I think Bihar's example would provide the stimulus and the movement—struggle and reconstruction, confrontation and cooperation—would spread.

IV

What I described yesterday (in Section III) may be only one way a movement for total change might spread to other States. But, there is another and more probable way perhaps. At the Gujarat and Bihar movements showed, it might grow out of a comparatively minor agitation and then spread like wildfire. In Gujarat, it began with agitation against a student's hostel warden and rapidly grew, forcing Mrs. Gandhi and the central government to compel the Gujarat Ministry to resign and finally dissolve the Assembly. Unfortunately, there was no one in Gujarat who could have carried forward the movement until at least its other aims had been achieved; removal of corruption, educational reform, solution of the problem of unemployment. For the students of Gujarat, it was a dazzling victory and no one can blame them for being dazzled by their success. That success and Morarjibhai's fast led to elections being held and the victory of the Janata front. This too was a great outcome of that struggle. But, like Chandra Shekhar, historians in the future might ask: "What was it all for? If that was all, why could they not wait unitl the next election?" This is one of Mrs. Gandhi's favourite propaganda themes.

Well, this question and this line of propaganda would have been quite valid had the Gujarat movement ended merely in replacing the Congress with the Janata Front in power. Superficially, it appears like this. But on deeper understanding the conclusion becomes inescapable that the Gujarat movement was a path-finder in India's march towards democracy, with a parliamentary democracy, in which the demos, the people, are not mere passive agents but are active, demanding and in the end commanding. The Gujarat movement established for the first time in India the primacy of the people, going over the heads of organised parties and asserting their will. True, it was the students and the youths who seemed to be manning the battle front, but without the support of the people behind them they could not have won. And the reason why the people backed the students was that the latter articulated the people's own grievances, desires and aims (no matter how vaguely formulated). India and Indian democracy will never be the same after the Gujarat movement. Having said all this, I must again repeat that it was a pity: (a) the Gujarat movement ended with the dissolution of the Assembly, and (b) no one is trying to utilise a friendly and responsive government to restart a revolutionary movement—call it a Navanirman movement or whatever—that could present an example of how there could be cooperation in place of confrontation in bringing about a total revolution in society.

I seem to have digressed from the main point I set out to make at the beginning. It is simply this, that no one can tell after Gujarat and Bihar what little spark anywhere may lead to a revolutionary movement in a State or in any area. The pre-conditions being present anywhere as in the two examples, it can begin and spread anywhere in the country. This is another, and a quite unpredictable, manner in which a Bihar-type movement may develop in other parts of India.

V

I remember Vinobaji saying to me, when he briefly broke his silence, that he agreed with my concept of struggle and was prepared to help me there, but that I should give up the idea of a struggle against the government. His objection to the latter struggle was that there was danger of war—in view of Pakistan's attitude, American supply of arms once again to Pakistan (the embargo having been lifted), and China's going out of the way to show its friendship for Pakistan. The struggle against the government might weaken the country. Vinobaji's did not apprehend that the struggle might end in the strangulation of Indian democracy.

The struggle, the movement, was for total revolution, i.e., revolution in every sphere of social life and organisation. The revolution being peaceful, it was not to happen suddenly and swiftly. It would take time, but the times being revolutionary, not too much time—perhaps a space of a decade or two. The basic systematic changes would happen first and the individual and group adaptations, mostly psychological, later.

This should make it clear that a revolutionary change of the political system was an integral and inescapable part of the total revolution and, therefore, of the struggle.

Perhaps Vinobaji held and still holds that systematic change in the political order could be brought about without a struggle, even a peaceful struggle. My experience of years of Gram Swarajya work has convinced me that Gram Swarajya is a valuable political organisation in itself, provided it works and is not only on paper. But, the Gram Swarajya movement was not capable of bringing about a systematic political revolution. Theoretically, there is no reason why it should not. I do not know at how many hundreds may be thousands, of meetings I had shown how, based on Gram Swarajya, the new polity would rise and displace the present one. I am not aware that any of my Sarvodaya colleagues, including those who are my severe critics now, ever found fault with my presentation. Districts were taken up, then C.D. (Community Development) blocks (as in the Saharsa district of Bihar) to build the model, but nowhere has success been achieved.

If we look at the task of total revolution from the narrow and doctrinaire (though never admitted as such) Sarvodaya point of view, it will be seen that the Gram Jana-Sangharsha Samitis (Village Committees for People's struggle) in Bihar were performing the same function as the *Gram Swarajya* and many of them were active and were not only on paper. As the struggle deepened, more and more of the Samitis would have become active and developed into real Janta Sarkars. The Gram Swarajya movement, beginning with Bhoodan and passing through Gramdan has taken more than twenty years to reach the ineffectual state in which it is found today.

On the other hand, the Gram Jana Sangharsha Samitis had hardly a few months in which to come to life and yet in many places they were much more real than Gram Swarajya. The reason I believe is the atmosphere of struggle. It seems to me that in such an atmosphere psychological forces are created that attract men and drive them to accept challenges and to change themselves and change others. In the placid atmosphere in which Gram Swarajya was working, such psychological forces remained dormant. Spiritual and moral appeals, the saintly influence of Vinobaji, did bring about some remarkable moral changes in some individuals. But they never became a social or psychological force. During the Bhoodan movement when hundreds of thousands of landlords donated their land, it might be claimed that a really widespread moral force, not confined to only a few, was created. Perhaps it was so. But, it was short-lived and later uncounted donors took back, or tried to take back, what they had given. That moral force was soon dissipated—though Vinobaji was still in the field and when Gramdan came along there was little of that force remaining. Some of the ideas about land and property remained, but not as accepted ideas. Had the latter been the case, those ideas could have become a tremendous force for social change.

It should not be deduced from the above that the atmosphere of struggle can be conjured up at will. It is only when the people generally, including the young and the students and the intelligentsia—and this latter is very important—are in a state of disaffection, frustration, disillusionment and are alienated from authority, that the conditions for a struggle are ripe. The struggle may break out in violence, or it may take a peaceful form. It need hardly be pointed out that a peaceful people's struggle for revolutionary change would be more acceptable in Gandhi's India than elsewhere, and would not appear in the eyes of the revolutionary activists as a chimera. In either case, leadership and organisation would be necessary to bring out of the revolutionary movement. In the absence of leadership and organisation, the revolutionary situation might end in chaos or imposition of a dictatorship.

VI

The question of the Bihar movement and other similar movements getting involved with opposition political parties has worried a number of friendly intellectuals and many well-wishers. I have been no less worried myself about it. As I look back I ask myself, did I make a mistake, and if so, what was it? I have asked myself this question again and again during the movement also. What were, and are, the answers? There is no doubt that if the movement had not got mixed up with Opposition parties, its character, its experimental utility, its educative value, its ability to enable the people to see their problems with their own eyes and to think of their responsibility to do whatever lay in their power to solve their problems, to change themselves and change their material and social environment, and if they must offer peaceful resistance or non-cooperation in this process, to do so singly, in groups or in 'mass' would not have been compromised.

But the ideal never gets translated into practice without suffering deterioration. The first difficulty was, and will be again whenever the attempt is made anew, that it is just not possible to keep political parties from coming into an open mass movement. True, if the movement had been confined to the Sarvodaya workers alone and its principle was to keep away all political parties, it would have been possible to keep them away. But, then, there would have been no people's movement.

Another aspect of this difficulty is that I did not start the movement. I had to take over what was on and give it direction, spread and depth. I am afraid, elsewhere and at other times other men wanting to build a people's movement will be faced with similar situations. Moreover, at its start, while the Bihar students movement was truly a non-party affair and 80 to 90 per cent of the young men and women who participated in its programme had no political party attachments, its leadership was surely made up of student and ex-student personnel who had strong party affiliations and who undoubtedly were guided by the party leaders outside. The parties involved were mainly four—Jana Sangh, Socialist party, B.L.D. and Congress (O). At several university centres the Jana Sangh was the strongest element, in some the B.L.D. and the S.P. The Congress (O) leadership in the Steering Committee was quite mature and influential, though numerically weak.

Now this was the situation when my association with the Bihar students movement started. The Political parties were there already. In fact, it will be admitted by all objective observers that my influence kept the party influence, low, helped to evolve a consensus, and give the movement at the start the students' movement and then the people's movement—a non-party political character.

There is yet another, and theoretically the most important, aspect of this problem of parties and a non-party people's movement. It is well known that both the Gujarat and Bihar movements started with certain demands or charges laid at the door of the State government: corruption, unemployment, educational reform plus minor complaints about examinations, admissions, hostels, etc. Now, as I have said earlier in these Notes, it was up to the State government to have met the students in a friendly manner and discussed the demands seriously and done something about them. But when in either State the government chose the path of confrontation, a struggle against the government became inevitable. The situation immediately attracted the opposition parties as honey attracts flies. What does one do in a situation like this? The conclusion from this is that an attempt should be made to avoid a confrontation with the government, as Vinobaji wanted me to do. The question is, can you do it? No one, at least no one who has no party affiliation, and therefore, no motivation to exploit every situation for partisan ends, and who still is anxious to start a peaceful revolutionary movement, i.e., a movement to bring about basic changes in society and in social attitudes, can ever, in the conditions of our country, avoid a confrontation with the kind of government we have. But if the miracle happens and the government and the ruling party come forward to cooperate with the revolutionary movement, that would be something to celebrate, not to mourn. But I do not see the Congress under Mrs. Gandhi ever behaving thus. What about the Opposition parties? Will they behave any better? That is to be seen. I personally think they will, at least, in Bihar and hopefully in other States too, provided there were in those States popular movements of change.

This brings me to the last part of this question.

Is the involvement of the political parties in a Bihar-type people's movement an unmixed evil? Its faults are obvious enough, as touched upon briefly in the foregoing and as articulated by every friendly and understanding critic. But in the first place, in an open movement involving the greater bulk of college students and the people, it is impossible to keep anyone out as I have shown above. After all, the parties that entered the movement in Bihar did not enter as parties, and their leaders, workers and sympathisers came in as individuals. These parties, of course, at their formal meetings outside the movement passed resolutions and issued statements fully supporting the movement. But, the question to aks is the participation of Opposition Parties an unmixed evil? My unhesitating answer is No. Its first result, too obvious be argued, is that it lends strength to the movement. But, the more important thing is that the parties undergo a sea-change in the process. True, this would not happen in a State where there is no strong non-party leadership in the movement. But in Bihar it.has happened. All the parties involved are committed to the aims of total revolution and to the dynamics of change: struggle. This is no small gain. And I would invite the consideration of my intellectual friends to this great possibility. So far, we have seen students' and people's struggle in the form of confrontation with the government. In Bihar, after the next elections there is every possibility of witnessing a people's struggle in cooperation with the State government. I hope the baptism of fire through which the Opposition has passed and is passing in Bihar would have steeled their commitement to total revolution. I admit, if God removes me from the scene before then, this will only remain a dream. But, the experience will not have been lost and later someone else will come forward to pick up the thread.

VII

I should add one thought to what I have written above. There is no possibility in sight and in the near future of India having any other type of democracy than she has today. Hopefully, if the Opposition wins the next parliamentary elections the present constitution and the electoral laws, etc., might be improved. But the 'type' of democracy will not change much. Therefore, there seems to be no way for a people's movement to carry forward its programmes of revolution except in the context of a party government. The context may be malignant or benign as discussed above.

In respect of 'improvement' in the present type of democracy. I have mentioned constitutional and statutory amendments under an opposition government. But there may be extra-constitutional and legal ways of doing it also. This can be possible only in the context of an on-going people's movement. These Struggle Committees or People's Committees, or Navanirman Samitis, Viplavi Samitis may perform, as we were aiming to do, and we shall again try to do so, the functions of (a) being sounding boards or consultation media at the time of candidate selection, and (b) acting as 'watch-dogs' and accountability-enforcers over their local representatives as well as over the whole working of the government.

BIBLIOGRAPHY

Adwani, B.T., *Influence of Socialism on Politics, Legislation and Administration in India Since Independence,* Sterling Publishers, New Delhi, 1975.

Ahuja, B.N., *J.P.: India's Revolutionary Number One,* Varma Publishing Company, Lahore, 1947.

Allan and Scarfe, *J.P.: His Biography,* Orient Longman, New Delhi, 1975.

Appadorai, A., *Indian Political Thinking in the Twentieth Century—Naoroji to Nehru: An Introductory Survey,* Oxford University Press, London, 1971.

Barik, R., *Politics of the J.P. Movement,* Radiant Publications, New Delhi, 1977.

Bali, D.R., *Modern Indian Thought from Ram Mohan Roy to M.N. Roy,* Sterling Publishers, Delhi, 1980.

Bhargava, G.S., *J.P.'s Jail Life,* Arnold Hunemann Publishers, New Delhi, 1977.

Bhattacharjee, A., *Jayaprakash Narayan: A Political Biography,* Vikas Publishing House, New Delhi, 1978.

Bright, J.S., *Life and Times of Jayaprakash Narayan,* Dewan Publications, Lahore, 1947.

Dutta, K.K., *History of the Freedom Movement in Bihar,* Vol. III, Government of Bihar, Patna, 1958.

Dutta, R., *India Today,* Manisha Granthalaya, Calcutta, 1970.

Gandhi, M.K., *Socialism of My Conception,* Bharatiya Vidya Bhavan, Bombay, 1957.

George, L., *The Origins of Socialism,* Weiderfield and Nicolson, London

Ghosh, A., *Theories and Practices of the Socialist Party of India,* People's Publishing House, Bombay, 1952.

Goyal, O.P., *Contemporary Indian Political Thought,* Kitab Mahal, Allahabad, 1965.

Graves, S., *History of Socialism,* The Horton Press, London, 1939.

Gupta, R.C., *J.P.: From Marxism to Total Revolution,* Sterling Publishing, New Delhi, 1981.

Jha, M.N., *Modern Indian Political Thought,* Meenakshi Prakashan, Meerut.

Karanjia, R.K., *Indira-J.P. Confrontation: The Great Debate,* Chetna Publishers, Delhi, 1975.

Kumarappa, B., *Capitalism, Socialism or Villagism,* S.S.S. Prakashan, Varanasi, 1965.

Lal, L.N., *Jayaprakash: Rebel Extraordinary,* Indian Book Company, Delhi, 1977.

Lal, M.B., *Principles of Socialism,* Tara Printing Press, Varanasi, 1965.

Lal, M.B., *Sarvodaya and Democratic Socialism,* Praja Socialist Publication, Varanasi

Mahajan, V.D., *Recent Political Thought,* S. Chand and Company, New Delhi, 1956.

Mahadevan, T.K., *Jayaprakash Narayan and the Future of Indian Democracy,* Affiliated East-West Press, New Delhi, 1975.

Masani, M., *Is J.P. the Answer?* Macmillan, Delhi, 1975.

Masani, M., *J.P. Mission Partly Accomplished,* The Macmillan Company, Delhi, 1977.

Mehta, A., *Socialism and Peasantry,* A Praja Socialist Party Publication, Bombay, 1953.

Narayan, J., *Why Socialism?* The All-India-Congress Socialist Party, Benaras, 1936.

Narayan, J., *Towards Struggle,* Padma Publications, Bombay, 1946.

Narayan, J., *The Socialist Way,* Dularelal Bhargava, Lucknow, 1946.

Narayan, J., *Political Trends, the Socialist Party,* Bombay, 1951.

Narayan, J., *Socialism to Sarvodaya,* Socialist Book Centre, Madras, 1956.

Narayan, J., *The Evolution Towards Sarvodaya,* Sarvodaya Prachuralaya, Tanjore, 1957.

Narayan, J., *From Socialism to Sarvodaya,* Akhil Bharat Sarva Seva Sangh Prakashan, Kashi, 1959.

Narayan, J., *The Dual Revolution,* A.B.S.S.S. Prakashan, Tanjore, 1959.

Narayan, J., *A Plea for Reconstruction of Indian Polity,* A.B.S.S.S. Prakashan, Kashi, 1959.

Narayan, J., *Swaraj for the People,* A.B.S.S.S. Prakashan, Varanasi, 1961.

Narayan, J., *Socialism, Sarvodaya and Democracy,* Asia Publishing House, Bombay, 1964.

Narayan, J., *Democratic Socialism: Our Ideal and Our Method,* Socialist Party, Bombay.

Narayan, J., *Is Violence An Alternative,* Navachetna Prakashan, Varanasi, 1973.

Narayan, J., *Communitarian Society and Panchayat Raj,* Navachetna Prakashan, Varanasi, 1970.

Narayan, J., *Three Basic Problems of Free India,* Asia Publishing House, Bombay, 1974.

Narayan, J., *On Parliamentary Democracy,* Nehru Memorial Museum and Library, New Delhi.

Narayan, J., *Total Revolution,* A.B.S.S.S. Prakashan, Varanasi, 1975.

Narayan, J. *Prison Diary,* Popular Prakashan, Bombay, 1977

Narayan, J., *Towards Total Revolution* Vol. I to Vol. IV, Popular Prakashan, Bombay, 1978.

Nargolkar, V., *J.P. Vindicated,* S. Chand & Company, New Delhi, 1977.

Prasad, R.A., *Socialist Thought in Modern India,* Meenakshi Prakashan, Meerut, 1974.

Seth, H.L., *The Red Fugutive: Jayaprakash Narayan,* Indian Printing Works, Lahore, 1944.

Sethi, J.D., *Gandhi Today,* Vikas Publishing House, New Delhi, 1978.

Sharma, M.L., *Gandhi: As a Socialist,* Deep and Deep Publication, New Delhi, 1980

Sharad, O., *Jayaprakash Narayan,* Sahitya Bhavan Private Limited, Allahabad, 1977

Sinha, S., *Socialism and Power,* Orient Longmans, Madras, 1974.

Singh, B., *The Political Ideas of M.N. Roy and Jayaprakash Narayan,* Ashish Publishing House, New Delhi, 1985.

Singh, H., *A History of the Praja Socialist Party. 1934-59,* Narendra Prakashan, Lucknow, 1959.

Tandon, P.D., *Leaders of Modern India,* Vora and Company Publisher, Bombay, 1955.

Tandon, V., *The Social and Political Philosophy of Sarvodaya After Gandhi,* S.S.S. Prakashan, Varanasi, 1965.

INDEX